A Year of Crochet Blankets

First published in the UK in 2027 by
Search Press Limited
Wellwood, North Farm Road,
Tunbridge Wells, Kent TN2 3DR

1 2 3 4 5 6 7 8 9 10

Original title: *Het Dekenfestijn van Haakplein*

First published by Kosmos Uitgevers, The Netherlands in 2024.
(Translation allowed.)
Text: Naomi Harreman and Jolanda Verschiere
Design and photography: Marissa van Roon
Editing: Katja Kaiser

English translation from the original Dutch edition
by Tankerton Translations.

ISBN: 978-1-80092-428-4
ebook ISBN: 978-1-80093-383-5

Bookmarked Hub

Extra copies of the patterns are available to download free from the Bookmarked Hub. Search for this book by title or ISBN: the files can be found under 'Book Extras'. Membership of the Bookmarked online community is free: www.bookmarkedhub.com

Publishers' notes

Metric measurements are used in this book; the imperial conversions are rounded to the nearest ¼in. Always use either metric or imperial measurements, not a combination of both.

US crochet terms are used throughout this book. For a list of UK equivalents please refer to page 8 and the inside front flap.

Yarns by Durable Yarn (www.durableyarn.com) and DMC (www.dmc.com) have been used in the creation of the projects in this book. If you are unable to source any of the yarns, please use the descriptions in the Materials lists as guidance for suitable alternatives.

The Publishers and authors can accept no responsibility for any consequences arising from the information, advice or instructions given in this publication.

For errata, please visit our website (www.searchpress.com) or the Bookmarked Hub (www.bookmarkedhub.com).

GPSR information can be found at www.searchpress.com
Printed in China, TT082026.

FSC www.fsc.org MIX Paper | Supporting responsible forestry FSC® C016973

A Year of Crochet Blankets

12 COZY DESIGNS IN A VARIETY OF COLOURS, PATTERNS AND STITCHES

NAOMI HARREMAN & JOLANDA VERSCHIERE

SEARCH PRESS

Naomi Harreman

Jolanda Verschiere

Preface

When we first met back in 2014, we never imagined that our hobby would take off in the way it has. We launched our first CAL (crochet-along) in 2016 – Mix 'n' Match 2016 – and since then our ideas have continued to flow. After a number of CALs and some stand-alone patterns, we were itching to bring together some of our designs into a book.

Not just CAL patterns, of course, but a real book. A book that had a lovely cover and beautiful photos, published by a proper publisher. And now our dream has come true!

This book contains entirely new patterns for colourful blankets, as well as beautifully simple and nostalgic bedspreads. Some patterns are a little trickier, while others are simple and relaxing to crochet. We've used cotton, as well as acrylic and mixed yarns throughout. All in all, it is a book packed full of information and inspirational designs that will hopefully provide you with many enjoyable hours of crocheting.

Contents

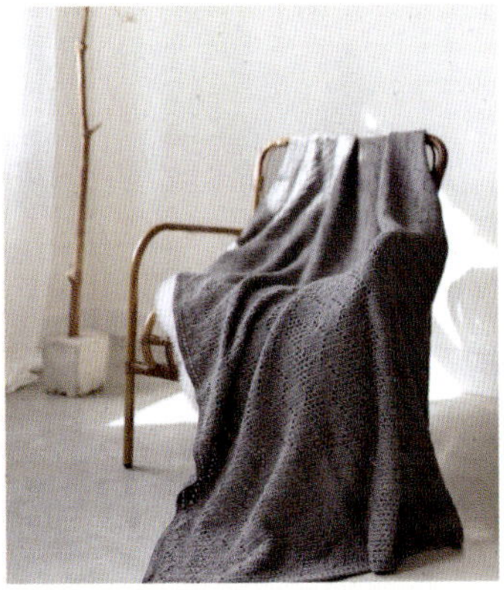

Abbreviations and crochet stitches used

*	repeat the pattern between * and *
( )	repeat a small part of the pattern
bo	bobble stitch
ch	chain
ch sp(s)	chain space(s)
cl2	2-dc cluster
cl3	3-dc cluster
dc	double crochet
dtr	double treble crochet
hdc	half double crochet
Ldtr	linked double treble crochet
Ltr	linked treble crochet
RS	right side of work
sc	single crochet
sk	skip
sl st	slip stitch
st(s)	stitch(es)
tog	together
tr	treble crochet
V-st	V-stitch
WS	wrong side of work
long tail foundation	
magic ring	

The patterns in this book use US crochet terminology. See the list below for UK equivalents.

US	UK
2-dc cluster (cl2)	2-tr cluster
3-dc cluster (cl3)	3-tr cluster
double crochet (dc)	treble crochet (tr)
double treble crochet (dtr)	triple treble crochet (ttr)
gauge	tension
half double crochet (hdc)	half treble crochet (htr)
magic ring	adjustable ring
single crochet (sc)	double crochet (dc)
skip	miss
treble crochet (tr)	double treble crochet (dtr)

Blankets... our secret pleasure

We love crocheting blankets. The best thing about blankets is that you always need one, whether it's spending a cool summer evening out on the patio, or for a perfect snuggle if you're feeling a little under the weather. You can make them as gifts for a newborn baby, for a wedding, or to bring some comfort for someone who is unwell.

A blanket is one of the easiest things to crochet. Fair enough, it might not be the smallest item you can crochet, but you can adapt it to any occasion, use your favourite yarn, and crochet in your favourite colours. Also, you don't have to worry about making it fit, like you do with clothes. It's normally quite easy to make the blanket bigger or smaller.

It's easy to adapt the blankets in this book to suit your needs. With each pattern, we've shown you how to widen and lengthen the blanket. You can do this by adding extra stitches in the set-up row or by adding extra stripes or blocks.

Just take a look on the internet and you'll discover there are *so* many different stitches you can use to make patterns – crocheting blankets will never get boring! We always end up finding lots of inspiration by scrolling through Pinterest.

And although that inspiration won't always immediately result in a new pattern, elements of it remain in our brains and we mull it over quietly until eventually, one day in the future, it becomes something tangible.

We've categorized the patterns in this book by three levels of difficulty: easy, medium, and difficult. That said, what one person finds easy, another person may think is quite challenging, and a very experienced crocheter might find our difficult patterns quite simple. We've tried to classify the patterns according to the whether *we* find them easy, medium, or difficult.

We sometimes use specific techniques such as the magic ring and the long tail foundation. If you are not familiar with these techniques, it's definitely a good idea to search for them on YouTube; Haakplein's channel is a good place to start. The long tail foundation is a really nice way to start, since you end up with a slightly stretchy foundation row, which is prettier than a chain of stitches. The magic ring is also a good alternative to working a number of chains that you join in a ring. Just don't forget to fasten off the magic ring properly. It might be called magic, but it can't perform miracles!

Our patterns also include repetitions. When we only want to repeat a small part of the pattern, we use (...). For larger sections, we use a *.

The round numbers are indicated in **BLUE** and **BLACK**. The blue round numbers are rounds that are crocheted on the right side of the work, while the black round numbers are crocheted on the wrong side of the work.

The stated sizes for the blankets in this book are all the sizes we ended up with when we crocheted them. If you crochet the blankets more tightly or loosely, you will end up with a smaller or larger blanket. That obviously means you will end up using more or less yarn to achieve the same finished size that we did.

We hope you will find that the patterns in this book fill you with inspiration to crochet your own blanket.

Note! *We cannot be held responsible if you run out of yarn or have too much left over if the blanket you make is not the original size, or if you crochet more loosely or tightly. The patterns include a clear indication of the amount of yarn that is needed.*

Basic stitches

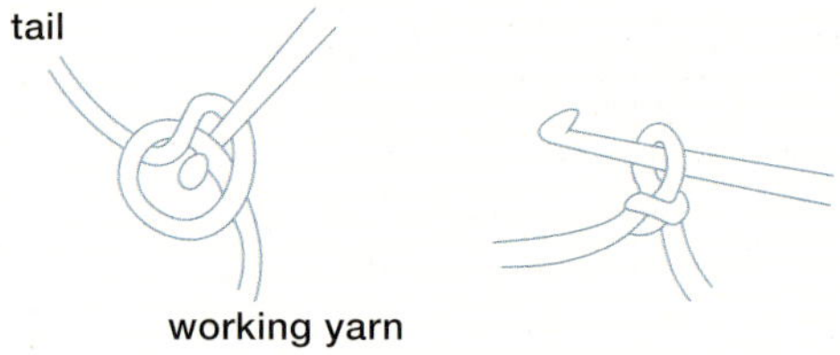

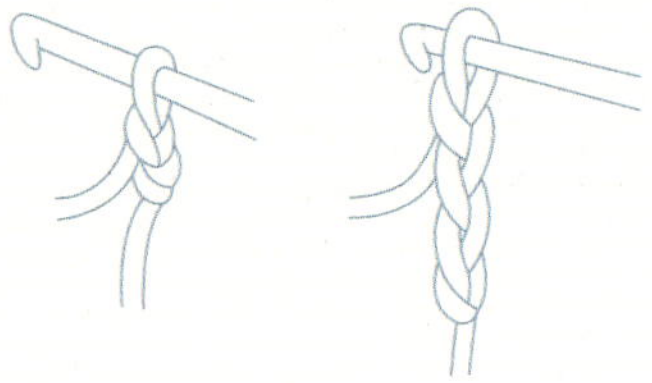

SLIP KNOT

Cross the working yarn over the tail of the yarn to make a loop. Insert your crochet hook through the loop and catch the working yarn. Pull it through the loop. Draw both the tail and the working yarn to tighten the slip knot, then pull the working yarn only to secure the knot on your hook.

CHAIN

Make a slip knot on your hook, leaving a tail of about 10cm (4in). Wrap the yarn clockwise over your crochet hook (known as 'yarn over'), and draw it through the first loop on your hook. You have now made one chain. Yarn over your crochet hook again and draw it through the loop on your hook. This is your next chain. Repeat this step as many times as needed until you have crocheted the required number of chains. This forms your foundation chain.

Work the following number of chains for each stitch at the beginning of a row:

sc = 1 ch
hdc = 2 ch
dc = 3 ch

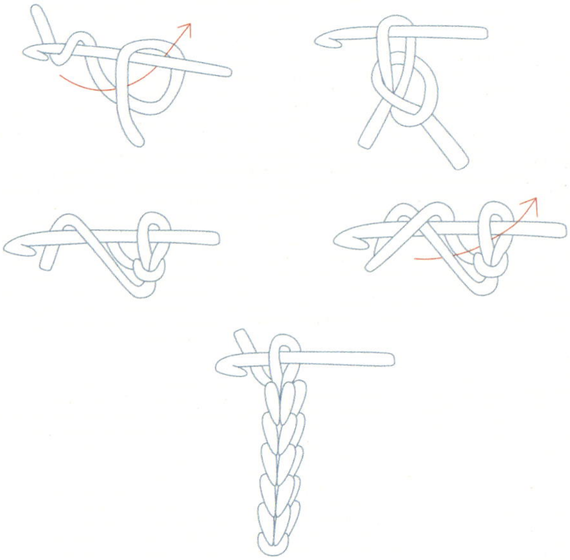

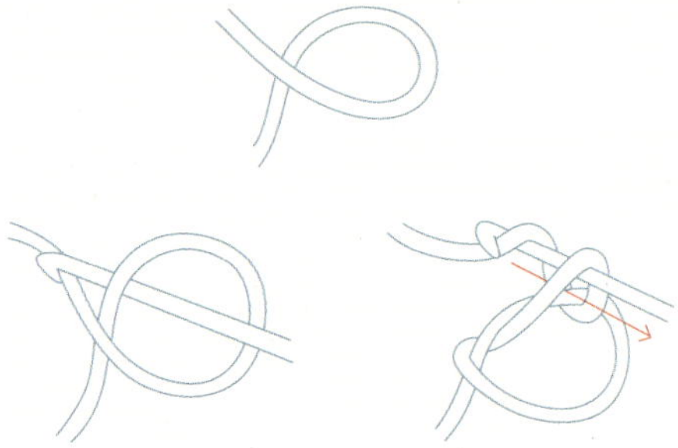

LONG TAIL FOUNDATION

Take a long piece of yarn (about three times the length of the chain you need) and start with a slip knot. Lay the ball of yarn at the back, with the working yarn laid over your index finger as if to crochet. Lay the tail of yarn over your thumb at the same time, then pinch the two yarns to your palm with your ring and pinky fingers. You should have made a slingshot shape with your hand. Yarn under with the tail, yarn over with the working yarn, then pull through both loops on the hook. Repeat as needed. Maintain a loose tension throughout.

MAGIC RING

Used for making round or shaped projects, a magic ring is a ring around which the first round of stitches is crocheted. To make a magic ring, cross the working yarn over the tail end of the yarn, as if to make a slip knot, but don't tighten the knot or loop. Instead, make a yarn over with the working yarn and pull it through the loop on your hook. You should have a ring secured by a chain stitch. At the end of the round, pull the short yarn tail from the magic ring and then tighten until it is the correct size. This will vary depending on the pattern.

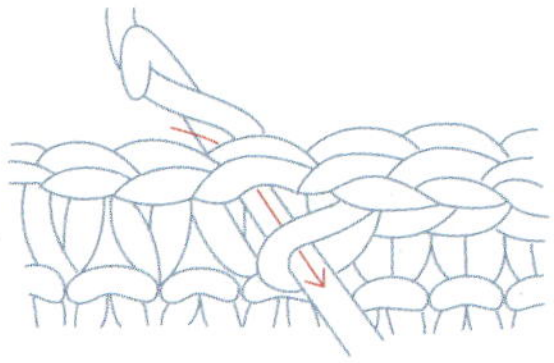

SLIP STITCH

Insert your hook in next stitch, yarn over and pull it straight through the stitch and the loop on your hook.

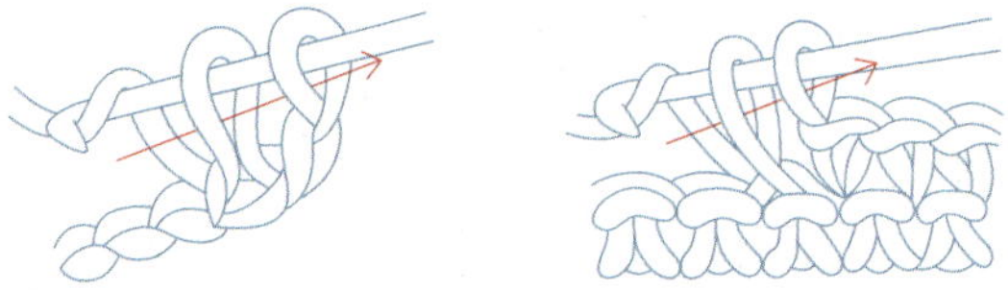

SINGLE CROCHET

Insert the crochet hook into the second chain or the next stitch from your hook. Yarn over and then pull it back through the stitch. Yarn over again and then pull it through both of the loops.

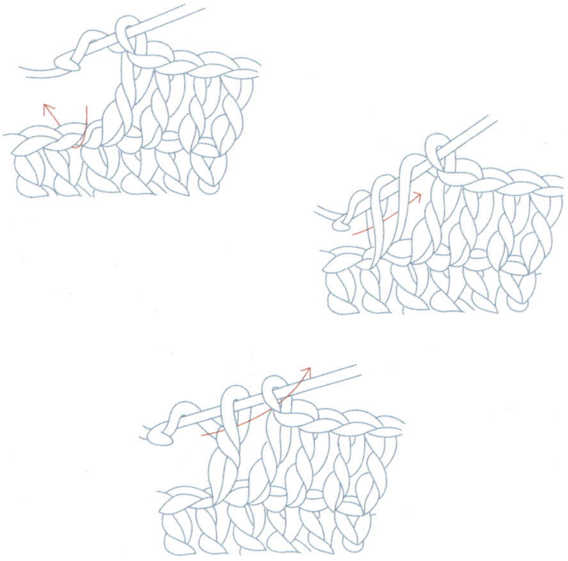

DOUBLE CROCHET

Yarn over hook and then insert the hook through the fourth chain or the next stitch. Yarn over hook again and then pull it back through the stitch. You now have three loops on your hook. Yarn over hook and pull it through the first two loops. Yarn over hook and pull it through the remaining two loops.

HALF DOUBLE CROCHET

Yarn over hook and then insert the hook through the third chain or the next stitch. Yarn over hook again and then pull it back through the stitch. You now have three loops on your hook. Yarn over hook and pull it through all of the loops that are on your hook at the same time.

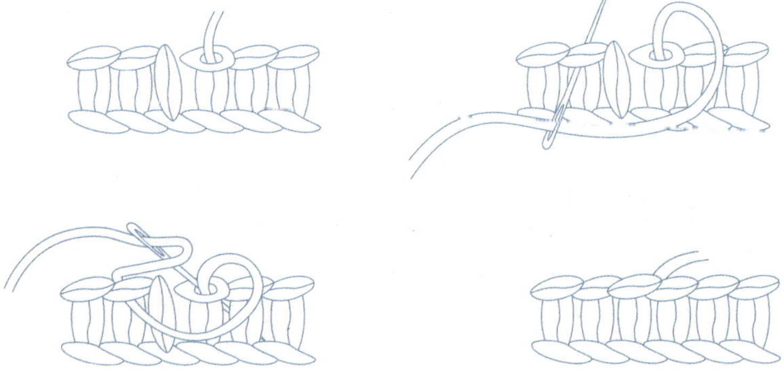

FASTEN OFF WITH YARN NEEDLE (NEEDLE JOIN)

1 Do this fasten-off at the end of the last round of a shape. Cut the yarn, keeping an end of about 10cm (4in) and then pull it through the last stitch. Make sure that the right side is facing you, then thread the end onto a yarn needle. Insert the needle under both loops of the first stitch after the turning chains of the round.

2 Insert the needle in the centre of the last stitch in the round. Pass the needle through to the wrong side and then complete the stitch to close the round. Weave the end of the yarn in the wrong side.

Floral Abundance

The hexagons that make up this blanket are crocheted in the fresh colours of spring, to form a cheerful flower garden.

Feel free to play around with the colours and create your own little garden.

MATERIALS

27 balls of **Durable Coral 4-ply (fingering) 100% cotton yarn** (50g/1¾oz/125m/137yd) in the following colours:

- 3 balls of Fresia/pink (239) (A)
- 2 balls of Rosa/pale pink (386) (B)
- 18 balls of White (310) (C)
- 2 balls of Light Green (2158) (D)
- 2 balls of Light Blue (282) (E)

TOOLS

2.5mm (US B-1/C-2, UK 13/12) crochet hook

Tapestry needle

FINISHED SIZE

1 block
25cm (10in) from corner to corner (diagonally)

Blanket
118 × 143cm (46½ x 56¼in)

DIFFICULTY LEVEL

Medium

PATTERN NOTES

The blanket is worked in the round from the RS throughout with no turning.

The first st in each round is created by working × ch, depending on the st that it replaces (e.g. dc = 3 ch). This is not in the written instructions.

STITCHES AND ABBREVIATIONS USED

bo	bobble; tr 5 together in same stitch or space
ch	chain(s)
ch sp(s)	chain space(s)
cl2	cluster; dc 2 together in same stitch or space
dc	double crochet
hdc	half double crochet
sc	single crochet
sk	skip
sl st	slip stitch
st(s)	stitch(es)
tog	together

ADDITIONAL STITCHES

MATTRESS STITCH

Arrange the pieces according to your chosen colour scheme, RS facing you. Insert the needle from bottom to top, through the back loop of the first stitch of the first (lower) triangle.

Then insert the needle from bottom to top and through the back loop of the first stitch of the second (upper) triangle.

Next, insert the needle from top to bottom-left and then through the back loop of stitch 1 to stitch 2 of the first (lower) triangle. Then, insert the needle from bottom to top-left and through the back loop of stitch 1 to stitch 2 of the second (upper) triangle.

Continue like this until you have formed 10 stitches in total; then carefully pull the yarn so that the seams close and the triangles lie tight against each other. Continue like this to the left corner chain stitch of both triangles. Fasten off.

KEY

– magic ring

– chain

– slip stitch

– single crochet

– double crochet

– cluster (dc 2 together worked into 1 stitch)

– bobble stitch (5 treble crochets worked into 1 stitch) – *see page 130*

HEXAGON

Make 28 hexagons: 6 using yarn E in centre, 6 using yarn D in centre, 6 using yarn B in centre, 10 using yarn A in centre.

Using yarn A, B, D or E, make a magic ring.

ROUND 1

(1 sc, ch 5) five times into ring, 1 sc into ring, ch 3, join with hdc in first sc (6 ch sps).

ROUND 2

Cl2 in first ch sp, ch 3, ([cl2, ch 3, cl2, ch 3] in next ch sp) five times, (cl2, ch 3) in next ch sp, join with a sl st (12 cl2).

ROUND 3

1 sl st in top of cl2, 1 sl st in ch sp, 1 sc in same ch sp, *(ch 1, 1 dc) four times in next ch sp, [ch 1, 1 sc] in next ch sp, rep from * four more times, (ch 1, 1 dc) four times in next ch sp, ch 1, join with a sl st (6 petals).

ROUND 4

1 sl st in first ch sp, 1 sl st in next st, *1 sc in next ch sp, ch 2, 1 sc in next ch sp, ch 2, 1 sc in same ch sp (place a marker in 2-ch sp), ch 2, 1 sc in next ch sp, ch 3, sk [1 dc, ch 1, 1 sc, ch 1, 1 dc], rep from * five more times, join with a sl st in first sc.

ROUND 5

1 sl st in 2-ch sp, cl2, *[ch 1, cl2, ch 3, cl2] in the marked 2-ch sp, [ch 1, cl2] in next 2-ch sp, [ch 1, cl2, ch 1, cl2] in next 3-ch sp**, [ch 1, cl2] in next 2-ch sp*, rep from * four more times, rep from * to ** once, ch 1, join with a sl st (6 cl2 per side).

Fasten off yarn, weave in ends.

ROUND 6

Join yarn C in any 3-ch sp, 2 dc in same 3-ch sp, *1 dc in each of next 11 sts and 1-ch sps along one side**, 3 dc in next 3-ch sp*, rep from * four more times, rep from * to ** once, 1 dc in 3-ch sp, join with a sl st (11 sts per side, 3 sts per corner).

Place a marker in centre stitch of each corner.

ROUND 7

[1 dc, ch 2, 1 dc] in first st, *(ch 1, sk 1 st, 1 dc in next st) six times, ch 1**, sk 1 st, [1 dc, ch 2, 1 dc] in centre dc of corner*, rep from * four more times, rep from * to ** once, join with a sl st (6 sts & 7 ch-sps per side, 2 sts & 1 ch sp per corner).

ROUND 8

1 sl st in corner sp, 2 dc in same ch sp, *1 dc in each st and ch sp along one side**, 3 dc in corner sp*, rep from * four more times, rep from * to ** once, 1 dc in first ch sp of previous round, join with a sl st (15 sts per side, 3 sts per corner).

Place a marker in centre stitch of each corner.

NOTE

In round 9, we will work with two colours. The bo will be made using the same colour as used for rounds 1 to 5. The rest of the sts will use yarn C. As you work, place the unused yarn along the top of the sts and crochet over it.

Change colour on the last yarn over of the dc before the bo and change back to yarn C on the last yarn over of the bo. These colour changes are not mentioned in the instructions.

ROUND 9

2 dc in first st, *1 dc in each of next 3 sts, bo in next st, (1 dc in each of next 4 sts, bo in next st) twice, 1 dc in each of next 3 sts**, 3 dc in marked st at corner*, rep from * four more times, rep from * to ** once, 1 dc in first st of previous round, join with a sl st (17 sts per side, 3 sts per corner).

Place a marker in centre stitch of each corner. Fasten off the coloured yarn.

ROUND 10

2 dc in first st, *1 dc in each st along one side**, 3 dc in marked st*, rep from * four more times, rep from * to ** once, 1 dc in first st of previous round, join with a sl st (19 sts per side, 3 sts per corner).

Place a marker in centre stitch of each corner.

ROUND 11

[1 dc, ch 2, 1 dc] in first st, *(ch 1, sk 1 st, 1 dc in next st) ten times, ch 1**, sk 1 st, [1 dc, ch 2, 1 dc] in middle dc of corner*, rep from * four more times, rep from * to ** once, join with a sl st (10 sts & 11 ch sps per side, 2 sts & 1 ch sp per corner).

Place a marker in 2-ch sp at each corner.

ROUND 12

1 sl st in corner sp, 2 dc in same ch sp, *1 dc in each st and ch sp along one side**, 3 dc in corner sp*, rep from * four more times, rep from * to ** once, 1 dc in first ch sp of previous round, join with a sl st (23 sts per side, 3 sts per corner).

Place a marker in centre stitch of each corner.

ROUND 13

2 dc in first st, *1 dc in each st along one side**, 3 dc in the marked st at corner*, rep from * four more times, rep from * to ** once, 1 dc in first marked st of the previous round, join with a sl st (25 sts per side, 3 sts per corner).

Fasten off and weave in the ends.

MAKING UP

Sew the blocks RS together using yarn C and mattress stitch, arranging them as shown in the top layout diagram on page 19.

Work the horizontal seams (orange line on the bottom diagram) first, paying attention to both the inside and outside corners, then sew the connecting seams (red lines on the bottom diagram).

BORDER

ROUND 1

Join yarn C to top right corner, 3 dc in corner (outside), 1 dc in each of next 27 sts, 3 dc in corner (outside), *1 dc in each of next 27 sts, dc3tog over middle dc of corner, seam line and middle dc of next corner (inside), rep from * once more, 1 dc in each of next 27 sts, 3 dc in corner (outside).

Continue all around in the same way (27 dc, then an inside or outside corner), join with a sl st.

ROUND 2

1 sl st in the middle st of corner, [1 dc, ch 2, 1 dc] in same st, (ch 1, sk 1 st, 1 dc in next st) fourteen times, ch 1, sk 1 st, (1 dc, ch 2, 1 dc) in next st, (ch 1, sk 1 st, 1 dc in next st) thirteen times, ch 1, sk 1 st, dc3tog over next 3 sts, (ch 1, sk 1 st, 1 dc in next st) twelve times, ch 1, sk 1 st, dc3tog over next 3 sts, (ch 1, sk 1 st, 1 dc in next st) thirteen times, ch 1, sk 1 st, (1 dc, ch 2, 1 dc) in next st, (ch 1, sk 1 st, 1 dc in next st) fourteen times, ch 1, sk 1 st, (1 dc, ch 2, 1 dc) in next st,

Continue all around in the same way, join with a sl st.

ROUND 3

1 sl st in corner sp, 3 dc in each outside corner 2-ch sp, dc3tog for each inside corner, 1 dc in each st and 1-ch sp around, join with a sl st.

ROUND 4

3 dc in each corner middle st, dc3tog for each inside corner, 1 dc in each st around, join with a sl st.

Fasten off and weave in the ends.

→

Hexagon Chart

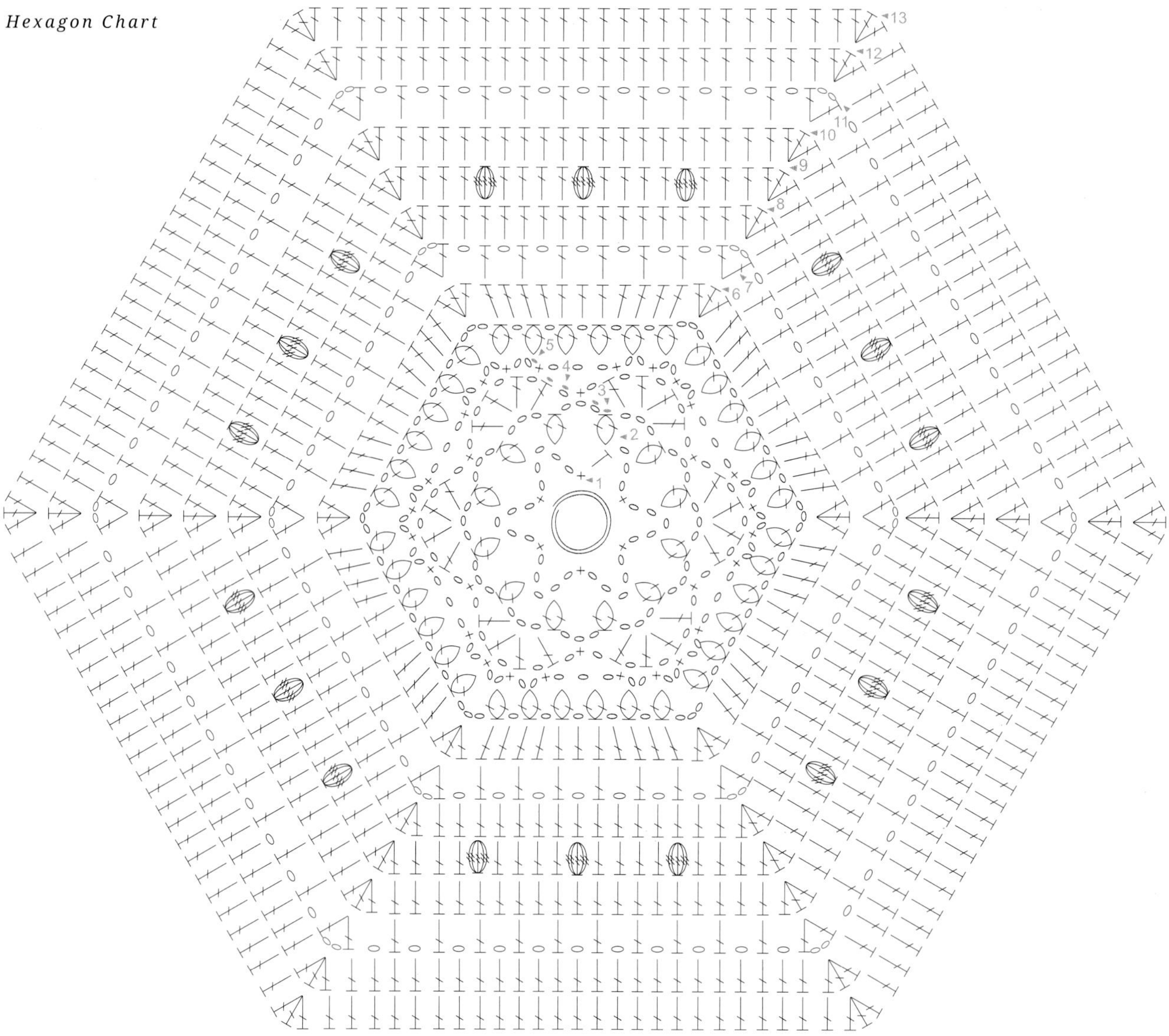

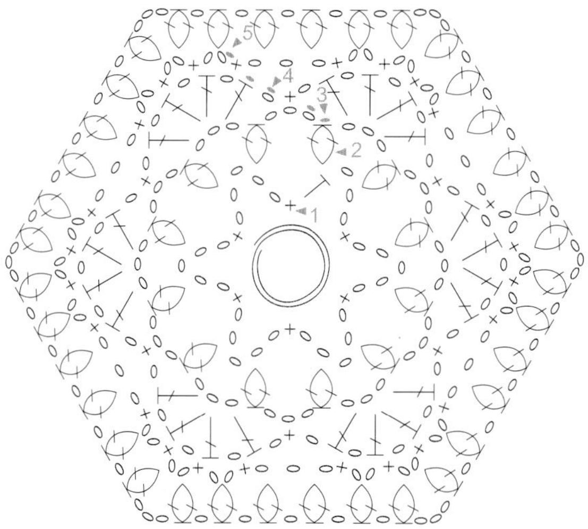

Joining Diagram A

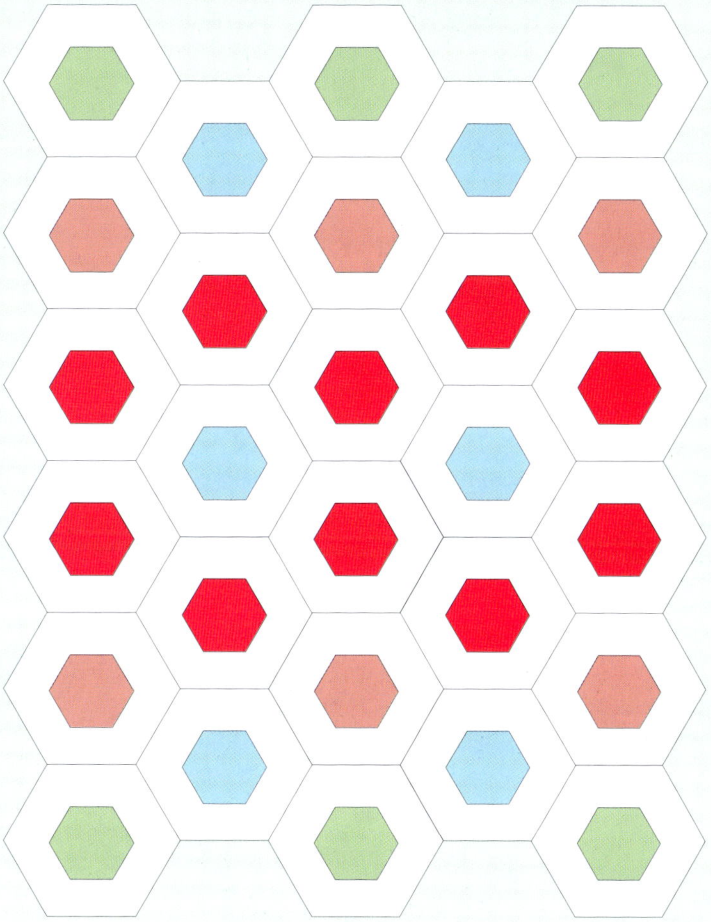

Joining Diagram B

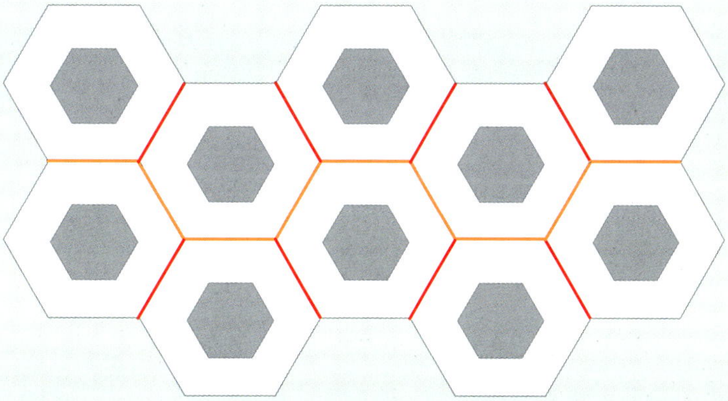

Border chart

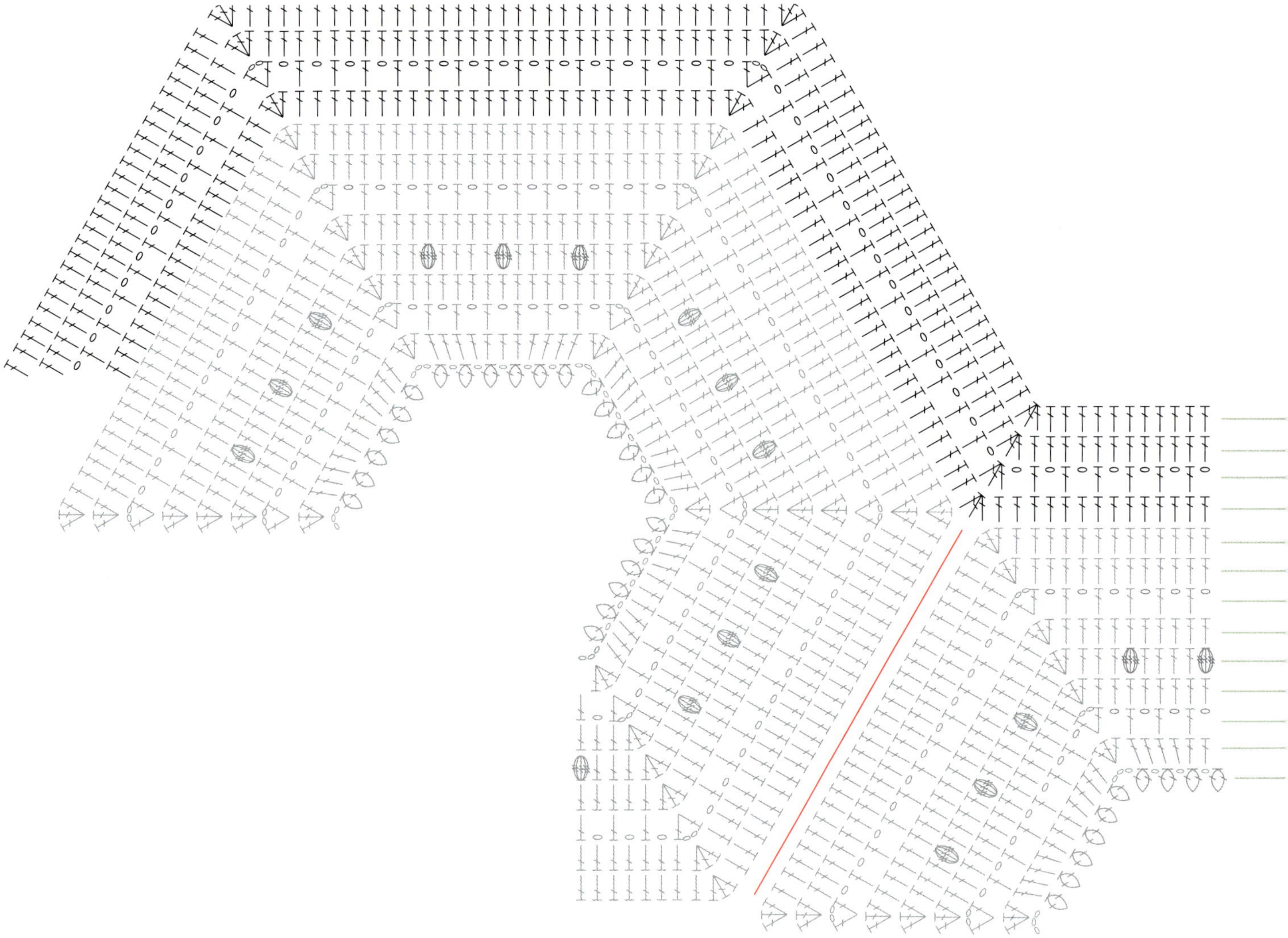

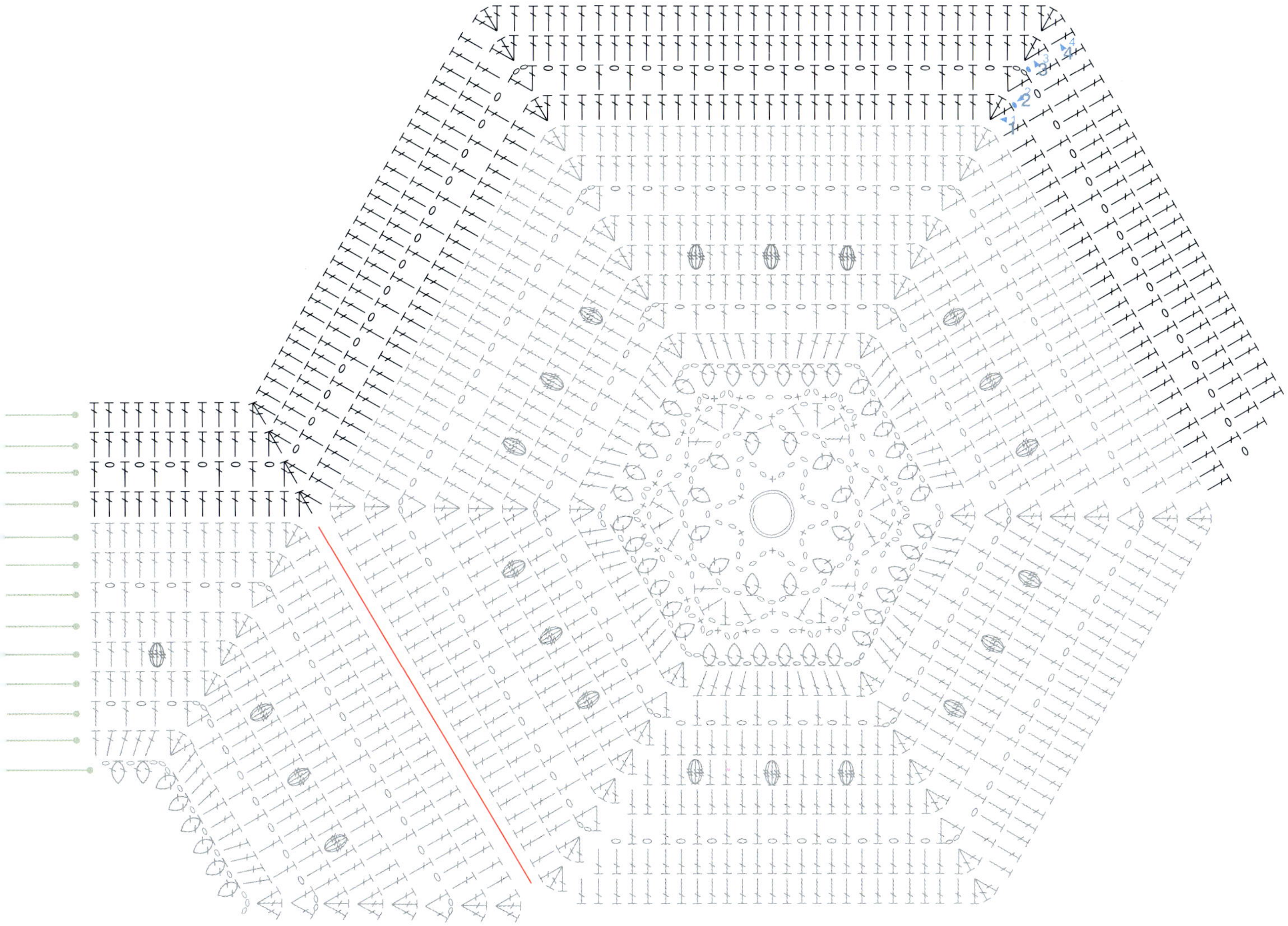

Kaleidoscope

Do you remember these vintage toys? Turning them around changes the pattern inside the kaleidoscope. This pattern is just like one of those reflections.

MATERIALS

21 balls of **Durable Comfy 5-ply (sport) microfibre acrylic yarn** (100g/3½oz/266m/290yd) in the following colours:

- 1 ball of Deep Fuchsia/dark pink (238) (A)
- 1 ball of Pink Lemonade/hot pink (242) (B)
- 1 ball of Light Pink (203) (C)
- 1 ball of Bright Mint (2136) (D)
- 1 ball of Atlantis/teal (342) (E)
- 1 ball of Cyan Blue (373) (F)
- 15 balls of Petrol/dark blue (375) (G)

TOOLS

One 3.5mm (US E-4, UK 9/10) crochet hook

Tapestry needle

FINISHED SIZE

1 triangle

Approx. 25 × 25 × 25cm (10 × 10 × 10in)

Blanket

Approx. 160 × 210cm (63 × 82½in)

DIFFICULTY LEVEL

Medium

PATTERN NOTES

The blanket is worked in the round from the front with no turning.

The first st in each round is created by working × ch, depending on the st that it replaces (e.g. dc = 3 ch). This is not in the written instructions.

STITCHES AND ABBREVIATIONS USED

ch	chain(s)
ch sp(s)	chain space(s)
cl3	cluster; dc 3 together in same stitch or space
dc	double crochet
sc	single crochet
sk	skip
sl st	slip stitch
st(s)	stitch(es)
tog	together
tr	treble crochet
V-st	V-stitch; tr, ch 2, tr in same stitch

ADDITIONAL STITCHES

TREBLE CROCHET (TR)

Yarn over hook twice, insert hook into next stitch or fifth chain from hook, yarn over; pull through; yarn over, pull through two loops, yarn over pull through two loops; yarn over pull through two loops.

CLUSTER3 (CL3) – DC

Yarn over hook, insert hook into next stitch, yarn over and pull through, yarn over and pull through two loops on hook, *yarn over, insert hook into same stitch, yarn over and pull through, yarn over and pull through two loops on hook, rep from * once more (four loops on hook), yarn over and pull through all loops on hook.

KEY

- *– magic ring*
- *– chain*
- *– slip stitch*
- + *– single crochet*
- *– double crochet*
- *– cluster (3 double crochets worked into 1 stitch)*
- *– V-stitch (treble crochet, chain 2, treble crochet in same stitch)*

TRIANGLE

Make 110 triangles: 20 each using yarn A, yarn B, yarn C, yarn D and yarn E for the first 3 rounds, and 10 triangles using yarn F for the first 3 rounds. The remaining rounds are worked in yarn C.

Using yarn A, B, C, D, E or F make a magic ring.

ROUND 1

(Cl3, ch 3) six times into ring, join with a sl st (6 cl3, 6 ch sps).

ROUND 2

1 sl st in 3-ch sp, ([cl3, ch 3, cl3, ch 3, cl3] in next ch sp, ch 3, 1 sc in next ch sp, ch 3) three times, join with a sl st (9 cl3, 12 ch sps).

ROUND 3

(1 dc in cl3, 4 dc in next ch sp, ch 5, 4 dc in next ch sp, 1 dc in next cl3, 2 dc in next ch sp, 1 dc in sc, 2 dc in next ch sp) three times, join with a sl st, changing to yarn G (15 sts each side, 3 ch sps).

Cut centre colour yarn.

ROUND 4

1 dc in each st, [3 dc, ch 5, 3 dc] in each 5-ch sp all around, join with a sl st (21 sts per side, 3 ch sps).

ROUND 5

(1 sc in dc, ch 3, sk 2 dc, 3 dc in next st, ch 3, sk 2 dc, 1 sc in next st, ch 3, sk 1 dc, [3 dc, ch 5, 3 dc] in 5-ch sp, ch 3, sk 1 dc, 1 sc in next st, ch 3, sk 2 dc, 3 dc in next st, ch 3, sk 2 dc, 1 sc in next st, ch 3, sk 2 dc, 3 dc in next st, ch 3, sk 2 dc) three times, join with a sl st (15 sts and 8 ch sps per side, 3 corner 5-ch sps).

ROUND 6

*(V-st in sc, ch 1, 1 dc in middle st of 3 dc, ch 1) twice, [3 dc, ch 5, 3 dc] in 5-ch sp, (ch 1, 1 dc in middle st of 3 dc, ch 1, V-st in sc) twice, ch 1, 1 dc in middle st of 3 dc, ch 1, rep from * twice more, join with a sl st (19 sts and 14 ch sps per side, 3 corner 5-ch sps).

ROUND 7

1 dc in each st, 1-ch sp and 2-ch sp, [3 dc, ch 5, 3 dc] in each 5-ch sp around, join with a sl st (39 sts per side, 3 corner 5-ch sps).

ROUND 8

1 dc in each st, [3 dc, ch 5, 3 dc] in 5-ch sp around, join with a sl st (45 sts per side, 3 corner 5-ch sps).

Fasten off and weave in ends.

Triangle Chart

Joining Diagram

NOTE

The numbers indicate the order in which to sew your blanket together.

Border Charts

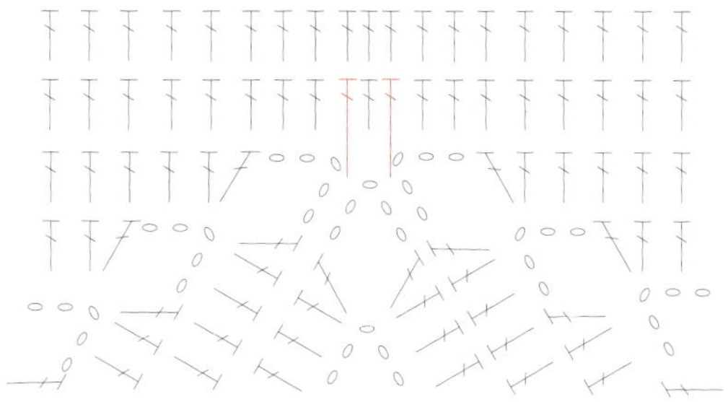

Top and bottom

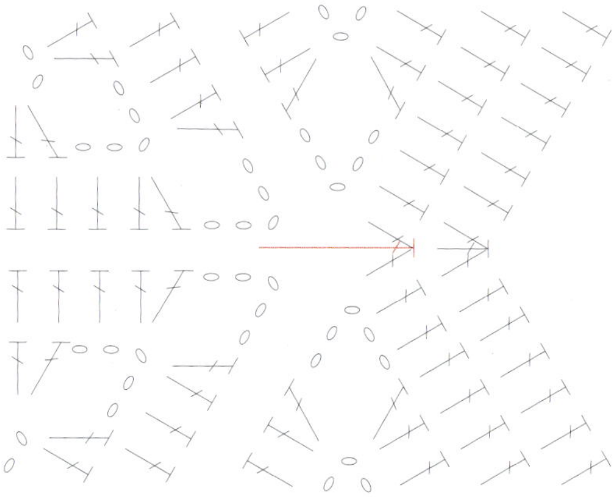

Inside corner

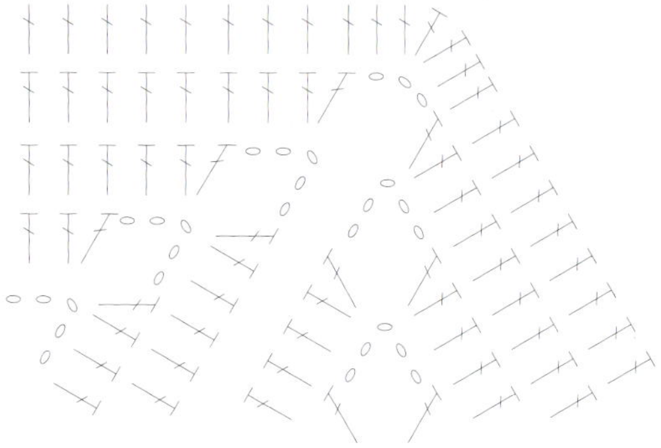

Outside corner

MAKING UP

Sew the triangles together with mattress stitch using yarn G according to the chart and layout diagram. Try to make the seams as long as possible so you don't have to fasten off and join in yarn too much.

The coloured lines on the chart show where to start, follow the numbered sequence of lines to join the top half of the blanket, then repeat for the bottom half.

BORDER

ROUND 1

Join yarn G to top right corner, *1 dc in each st along edge of one triangle, where 3 triangles meet work [2 dc in ch sp, 1 dc in seam, 1 dc in second ch sp, 1 dc in next seam, 2 dc in third ch sp], rep from * along top edge, 1 dc in each st along top edge of last triangle, in top left outer corner work [3 dc in ch sp, ch 3, sk the seam, 3 dc in next ch sp].

Continue in this way around, at the inside corners along the side edges work [2 dc in the first ch sp, dc3tog over, first ch sp, middle seam, last ch sp, 2 dc into the last ch sp].

When complete join with a sl st.

ROUND 2

1 dc in each st, in the outside corners work 5 dc in the ch sp, in the inside corners work dc3tog over (st before dc3tog, next st, st after dc3tog).

Continue in this way around, when complete join with a sl st.

Fasten off and weave in the ends.

Layout Diagram

Woven Harmony

The woven design harmonizes beautifully with the filet squares and spider-web shapes that appear in this pattern.

MATERIALS

15 balls of **DMC Knitty 4 DK (8-ply/light worsted) acrylic yarn** (100g/3½oz/280m/306yd) in Rose (851)

TOOLS

4mm (US J-6, UK 8) crochet hook

FINISHED SIZE

Approx. 160 × 230cm (63 × 91in)

DIFFICULTY LEVEL

Medium

PATTERN NOTES

The blanket is worked in rows, and you will need to turn the work at the end of each row. These turns are not included in the written instructions.

Work 3 ch for the turning chain at the beginning of each row. Note that this is not stated in the written instructions. This means, for example, that if you start a row with 3 dc, you will work one 3-ch then 2 dc.

STITCHES AND ABBREVIATIONS USED

ch	chain(s)
ch sp(s)	chain space(s)
cl2	cluster, dc 2 together in same stitch or space
dc	double crochet
dtr	double treble crochet
RS	right side of work
sc	single crochet
sk	skip
sl st	slip stitch
st(s)	stitch(es)
tog	together
WS	wrong side of work

ADDITIONAL STITCHES

DOUBLE TREBLE CROCHET (DTR)
Yarn over hook three times, insert hook into next stitch or fith chain, yarn over and pull through (yarn over and pull through two loops on hook) four times.

KEY

- *– long tail foundation*
- *– chain*
- *– single crochet*
- *– double crochet*
- *– double treble crochet*
- *– cluster (2 double crochets worked into 1 stitch)*

Make 275 sts using long tail foundation.

ROW 1 (RS)

1 dc in each st (275 sts).

ROW 2 (WS)

1 dc in each of first 3 sts, (ch 1, sk 1 st, 1 dc in next st) seven times, cl2 in next st, 1 dc in next st, (ch 7, sk 6 sts, 2 sc in next st, 1 sc in each of next 3 sts, 2 sc in next st, ch 7, sk 6 sts, 1 dc in next st, cl2 in next st, 1 dc in next st, ch 1, sk 1 st, 1 dc in each of next 15 sts, ch 1, sk 1 st, 1 dc in next st, cl2 in next st, 1 dc in next st) twice, ch 7, sk 6 sts, 2 sc in next st, 1 sc in each of next 3 sts, 2 sc in next st, ch 7, sk 6 sts, 1 dc in next st, cl2 in next st, 1 dc in next st, (ch 1, sk 1 st, 1 dc in next st) nine times, cl2 in next st, 1 dc in next st, (ch 1, sk 1 st, 1 dc in next st) nine times, cl2 in next st, 1 dc in next st, (ch 7, sk 6 sts, 2 sc in next st, 1 sc in each of next 3 sts, 2 sc in next st, ch 7, sk 6 sts, 1 dc in next st, cl2 in next st, 1 dc in next st, ch 1, sk 1 st, 1 dc in each of next 15 sts, ch 1, sk 1 st, 1 dc in next st, cl2 in next st, 1 dc in next st) twice, ch 7, sk 6 sts, 2 sc in next st, 1 sc in each of next 3 sts, 2 sc in next st, ch 7, sk 6 sts, 1 dc in next st, cl2 in next st, 1 dc in next st, (ch 1, sk 1 st, 1 dc in next st) seven times, 1 dc in each of last 2 sts.

ROW 3

1 dc in each of first 3 sts, (ch 1, sk ch 1, 1 dc in next st) six times, cl2 in ch sp, 1 dc in next st, ch 1, sk cl2, 1 dc in next st, [cl2, 1 dc] in ch sp, (ch 7, 1 sc in each of middle 5 sc, ch 7, [1 dc, cl2] in ch sp, 1 dc in next st, ch 1, sk cl2, 1 dc in each of next 15 sts, ch 1, sk 1 dc, 1 dc in next st, cl2 in ch sp, 1 dc in next st, ch 1, sk cl2, 1 dc in next st, [cl2, 1 dc] in ch sp) twice, ch 7, 1 sc in each of middle 5 sc, ch 7, [1 dc, cl2] in ch sp, 1 dc in next st, (ch 1, sk 1 st, 1 dc in next st) nine times, cl2 in ch sp, 1 dc in next st, ch 1, sk cl2, 1 dc in next st, cl2 in ch sp, 1 dc in next st, (ch 1, sk 1 st, 1 dc in next st) nine times, [cl2, 1 dc] in ch sp, (ch 7, 1 sc in each of middle 5 sc, ch 7, [1 dc, cl2] in ch sp, 1 dc in next st, ch 1, sk cl2, 1 dc in next st, cl2 in ch sp, 1 dc in next st, ch 1, sk 1 st, 1 dc in each of next 15 sts, ch 1, sk cl2, 1 dc in next st, [cl2, 1 dc] in ch sp) twice, ch 7, 1 sc in each of middle 5 sc, ch 7, [1 dc, cl2] in ch sp, 1 dc in next st, ch 1, sk cl2, 1 dc in next st, cl2 in ch sp, 1 dc in next st, (ch 1, sk ch 1, 1 dc in next st) six times, 1 dc in each of last 2 dc.

ROW 4

1 dc in each of first 3 sts, (ch 1, sk ch 1, 1 dc in next st) five times, cl2 in ch sp, 1 dc in next st, (ch 5, sk [cl2, 1 dc], 1 dtr in ch sp, ch 5, sk [1 dc, cl2], 1 dc in next st, [cl2, 1 dc] in ch sp, ch 5, 1 sc in each of middle 3 sc, ch 5, [1 dc, cl2] in ch sp, 1 dc in next st, ch 1, sk cl2, 1 dc in each of next 15 sts, ch 1, sk 1 dc, 1 dc in next st, cl2 in ch sp, 1 dc in next st) twice, ch 5, sk [cl2, 1 dc], 1 dtr in ch sp, ch 5, sk [1 dc, cl2], 1 dc in next st, [cl2, 1 dc] in ch sp, ch 5, 1 sc in each of middle 3 sc, ch 5, [1 dc, cl2] in ch sp, 1 dc in next st, (ch 1, sk 1 st, 1 dc in next st) nine times, cl2 in ch sp, 1 dc in next st, ch 5, sk [cl2, 1 dc], 1 dtr in ch sp, ch 5, sk [1 dc, cl2], 1 dc in next st, cl2 in ch sp, 1 dc in next st, (ch 1, sk 1 st, 1 dc in next st) nine times, [cl2, 1 dc] in ch sp, (ch 5, 1 sc in each of middle 3 sc, ch 5, [1 dc, cl2] in ch sp, 1 dc in next st, ch 5, sk [cl2, 1 dc], 1 dtr in ch sp, ch 5, sk [1 dc, cl2], 1 dc in next st, cl2 in ch sp, 1 dc in next st, ch 1, sk 1 dc, 1 dc in each of next 15 sts, ch 1, sk cl2, 1 dc in next st, [cl2, 1 dc] in ch sp) twice, ch 5, 1 sc in each of middle 3 sc, ch 5, [1 dc, cl2] in ch sp, 1 dc in next st, ch 5, sk [cl2, 1 dc], 1 dtr in ch sp, ch 5, sk [1 dc, cl2], 1 dc in next st, cl2 in ch sp, 1 dc in next st, (ch 1, sk ch 1, 1 dc in next st) five times, 1 dc in each of last 2 sts.

ROW 5

1 dc in each of first 3 sts, (ch 1, sk ch 1, 1 dc in next st) four times, cl2 in ch sp, 1 dc in next st, (ch 5, sk [cl2, 1 dc], 1 sc in ch sp, 1 sc in dtr, 1 sc in ch sp, ch 5, sk [1 dc, cl2], 1 dc in next st, [cl2, 1 dc] in ch sp, ch 3, 1 dtr in middle sc, ch 3, [1 dc, cl2] in ch sp, 1 dc in next st, ch 1, sk cl2, 1 dc in each of next 15 sts, ch 1, sk 1 dc, 1 dc in next st, cl2 in ch sp, 1 dc in next st) twice, ch 5, sk [cl2, 1 dc], 1 sc in ch sp, 1 sc in dtr, 1 sc in ch sp, ch 5, sk [1 dc, cl2], 1 dc in next st, [cl2, 1 dc] in ch sp, ch 3, 1 dtr in middle sc, ch 3, [1 dc, cl2] in ch sp, 1 dc in next st, (ch 1, sk 1 st, 1 dc in next st) nine times, cl2 in ch sp, 1 dc in next st, ch 5, sk [cl2, 1 dc], 1 sc in ch sp, 1 sc in dtr, 1 sc in ch sp, ch 5, sk [1 dc, cl2], 1 dc in next st, cl2 in ch sp, 1 dc in next st, (ch 1, sk 1 st, 1 dc in next st) nine times, [cl2, 1 dc] in ch sp, (ch 3, 1 dtr in middle sc, ch 3, [1 dc, cl2] in ch sp, 1 dc in next st, ch 5, sk [cl2, 1 dc], 1 sc in ch sp, 1 sc in dtr, 1 sc in ch sp, ch 5, sk [1 dc, cl2], 1 dc in next st, cl2 in ch sp, 1 dc in next st, ch 1, sk 1 dc, 1 dc in each of next 15 sts, ch 1, sk cl2, 1 dc in next st, [cl2, 1 dc] in ch sp) twice, ch 3, 1 dtr in middle sc, ch 3, [1 dc, cl2] in ch sp, 1 dc in next st, ch 5, sk [cl2, 1 dc], 1 sc in ch sp, 1 sc in dtr, 1 sc in ch sp, ch 5, sk [1 dc, cl2], 1 dc in next st, cl2 in ch sp, 1 dc in next st, (ch 1, sk ch 1, 1 dc in next st) four times, 1 dc in each of last 2 dc.

ROW 6

1 dc in each of first 3 sts, (ch 1, sk ch 1, 1 dc in next st) three times, cl2 in ch sp, 1 dc in next st, (ch 6, sk [cl2, 1 dc], 1 sc in ch sp, 1 sc in each of middle 3 sc, 1 sc in ch sp, ch 6, sk [1 dc, cl2], 1 dc in next st, [cl2, 1 dc] in ch sp, ch 1, sk dtr, [1 dc, cl2] in ch sp, 1 dc in next st, ch 1, sk cl2, 1 dc in each of next 15 sts, ch 1, sk 1 dc, 1 dc in next st, cl2 in ch sp, 1 dc in next st) twice, ch 6, sk [cl2, 1 dc], 1 sc in ch sp, 1 sc in each of middle 3 sc, 1 sc in ch sp, ch 6, sk [1 dc, cl2], 1 dc in next st, [cl2, 1 dc] in ch sp, ch 1, sk dtr, [1 dc, cl2] in ch sp, 1 dc in next st, (ch 1, sk 1 st, 1 dc in next st) nine times, cl2 in ch sp, 1 dc in next st, ch 6, sk [cl2, 1 dc], 1 sc in ch sp, 1 sc in each of middle 3 sc, 1 sc in ch sp, ch 6, sk [1 dc, cl2], 1 dc in next st, cl2 in ch sp, 1 dc in next st, (ch 1, sk 1 st, 1 dc in next st) nine times, [cl2, 1 dc] in ch sp, (ch 1, sk dtr, [1 dc, cl2] in ch sp, 1 dc in next st, ch 6, sk [cl2, 1 dc], 1 sc in ch sp, 1 sc in each of middle 3 sc, 1 sc in ch sp, ch 6, sk [1 dc, cl2], 1 dc in next st, cl2 in ch sp, 1 dc in next st, ch 1, sk 1 dc, 1 dc in each of next 15 sts, ch 1, sk cl2, 1 dc in next st, [cl2, 1 dc] in ch sp) twice, ch 1, sk dtr, [1 dc, cl2] in ch sp, 1 dc in next st, ch 6, sk [cl2, 1 dc], 1 sc in ch sp, 1 sc in each of middle 3 sc, 1 sc in ch sp, ch 6, sk [1 dc, cl2], 1 dc in next st, cl2 in ch sp, 1 dc in next st, (ch 1, sk ch 1, 1 dc in next st) three times, 1 dc in each of last 2 dc.

ROW 7

1 dc in each of first 3 sts, (ch 1, sk ch 1, 1 dc in next st) twice, cl2 in ch sp, 1 dc in next st, (ch 7, sk [cl2, 1 dc], 1 sc in ch sp, 1 sc in each of middle 5 sc, 1 sc in ch sp, ch 7, sk [1 dc, cl2], 1 dc in next st, cl2 in ch sp, 1 dc in next st, ch 1, sk cl2, 1 dc in each of next 15 sts, ch 1, sk 1 dc, 1 dc in next st, cl2 in ch sp, 1 dc in next st) twice, ch 7, sk [cl2, 1 dc], 1 sc in ch sp, 1 sc in each of middle 5 sc, 1 sc in ch sp, ch 7, sk [1 dc, cl2], 1 dc in next st, cl2 in ch sp, 1 dc in next st, (ch 1, sk 1 st, 1 dc in next st) nine times, cl2 in ch sp, 1 dc in next st, ch 7, sk [cl2, 1 dc], 1 sc in ch sp, 1 sc in each of middle 5 sc, 1 sc in ch sp, ch 7, sk [1 dc, cl2], 1 dc in next st, cl2 in ch sp, 1 dc in next st, (ch 1, sk 1 st, 1 dc in next st) nine times, cl2 in ch sp, 1 dc in next st, (ch 7, sk [cl2, 1 dc], 1 sc in ch sp, 1 sc in each of middle 5 sc, 1 sc in ch sp, ch 7, sk [1 dc, cl2], 1 dc in next st, cl2 in ch sp, 1 dc in next st, ch 1, sk 1 dc, 1 dc in each of next 15 sts, ch 1, sk cl2, 1 dc in next st, cl2 in ch sp, 1 dc in next st) twice, ch 7, sk [cl2, 1 dc], 1 sc in ch sp, 1 sc in each of middle 5 sc, 1 sc in ch sp, ch 7, sk [1 dc, cl2], 1 dc in next st, cl2 in ch sp, 1 dc in next st, (ch 1, sk ch 1, 1 dc in next st) twice, 1 dc in each of last 2 dc.

ROW 8

1 dc in each of first 3 sts, (ch 1, sk ch 1, 1 dc in next st) three times, [cl2, 1 dc] in ch sp, (ch 7, 1 sc in each of middle 5 sc, ch 7, [1 dc, cl2] in ch sp, 1 dc in next st, ch 1, sk cl2, 1 dc in next st, cl2 in ch sp, 1 dc in next st, ch 1, sk 1 dc, 1 dc in each of next 15 sts, ch 1, sk cl2, 1 dc in next st, [cl2, 1 dc] in ch sp) twice, ch 7, 1 sc in each of middle 5 sc, ch 7, [1 dc, cl2] in ch sp, 1 dc in next st, ch 1, sk cl2, 1 dc in next st, cl2 in ch sp, 1 dc in next st, (ch 1, sk 1 st, 1 dc in next st) nine times, [cl2, 1 dc] in ch sp, ch 7, 1 sc in each of middle 5 sc, ch 7, [1 dc, cl2] in ch sp, 1 dc in next st, (ch 1, sk 1 st, 1 dc in next st) nine times, cl2 in ch sp, 1 dc in next st, (ch 1, sk cl2, 1 dc in next st, [cl2, 1 dc] in ch sp, ch 7, 1 sc in each of middle 5 sc, ch 7, [1 dc, cl2] in ch sp, 1 dc in next st, ch 1, sk cl2, 1 dc in each of next 15 sts, ch 1, sk 1 dc, 1 dc in next st, cl2 in ch sp, 1 dc in next st) twice, ch 1, sk cl2, 1 dc in dc, [cl2, 1 dc] in ch sp, ch 7, 1 sc in each of middle 5 sc, ch 7, [1 dc, cl2] in ch sp, 1 dc in next st, (ch 1, sk 1 st, 1 dc in next st) three times, 1 dc in each of last 2 dc.

ROW 9

1 dc in each of first 3 sts, (ch 1, sk ch 1, 1 dc in next st) four times, [cl2, 1 dc] in ch sp, (ch 5, 1 sc in each of middle 3 sc, ch 5, [1 dc, cl2] in ch sp, 1 dc in next st, ch 5, sk [cl2, 1 dc], 1 dtr in ch sp, ch 5, sk [1 dc, cl2], 1 dc in next st, cl2 in ch sp, 1 dc in next st, ch 1, sk 1 dc, 1 dc in each of next 15 sts, ch 1, sk cl2, 1 dc in next st, [cl2, 1 dc] in ch sp) twice, ch 5, 1 sc in each of middle 3 sc, ch 5, [1 dc, cl2] in ch sp, 1 dc in next st, ch 5, sk [cl2, 1 dc], 1 dtr in ch sp, ch 5, sk [1 dc, cl2], 1 dc in next st, cl2 in ch sp, 1 dc in next st, (ch 1, sk 1 st, 1 dc in next st) nine times, [cl2, 1 dc] in ch sp, ch 5, 1 sc in each of middle 3 sc, ch 5, [1 dc, cl2] in ch sp, 1 dc in next st, (ch 1, sk 1 st, 1 dc in next st) nine times, cl2 in ch sp, 1 dc in next st, (ch 5, sk [cl2, 1 dc], 1 dtr in ch sp, ch 5, sk [1 dc, cl2], 1 dc in next st, [cl2, 1 dc] in ch sp, ch 5, 1 sc in each of middle 3 sc, ch 5, [1 dc, cl2] in ch sp, 1 dc in next st, ch 1, sk cl2, 1 dc in each of next 15 sts, ch 1, sk 1 dc, 1 dc in next st, cl2 in ch sp, 1 dc in next st) twice, ch 5, sk [cl2, 1 dc], 1 dtr in ch sp, ch 5, sk [1 dc, cl2], 1 dc in next st, [cl2, 1 dc] in ch sp, ch 5, 1 sc in each of middle 3 sc, ch 5, [1 dc, cl2] in ch sp, 1 dc in next st, (ch 1, sk 1 st, 1 dc in next st) four times, 1 dc in each of last 2 dc.

ROW 10

1 dc in each of first 3 sts, (ch 1, sk ch 1, 1 dc in next st) five times, [cl2, 1 dc] in ch sp, (ch 3, 1 dtr in next sc, ch 3, [1 dc, cl2] in ch sp, 1 dc in next st, ch 5, sk [cl2, 1 dc], 1 sc in ch sp, 1 sc in dtr, 1 sc in ch sp, ch 5, sk [1 dc, cl2], 1 dc in next st, cl2 in ch sp, 1 dc in next st, ch 1, sk 1 dc, 1 dc in each of next 15 sts, ch 1, sk cl2, 1 dc in next st, [cl2, 1 dc] in ch sp) twice, ch 3, 1 dtr in next sc, ch 3, [1 dc, cl2] in ch sp, 1 dc in next st, ch 5, sk [cl2, 1 dc], 1 sc in ch sp, 1 sc in dtr, 1 sc in ch sp, ch 5, sk [1 dc, cl2], 1 dc in next st, cl2 in ch sp, 1 dc in next st, (ch 1, sk 1 st, 1 dc in next st) nine times, [cl2, 1 dc] in ch sp, ch 3, 1 dtr in next sc, ch 3, [1 dc, cl2] in ch sp, 1 dc in next st, (ch 1, sk 1 st, 1 dc in next st) nine times, cl2 in ch sp, 1 dc in next st, (ch 5, sk [cl2, 1 dc], 1 sc in ch sp, 1 sc in dtr, 1 sc in ch sp, ch 5, sk [1 dc, cl2], 1 dc in next st, [cl2, 1 dc] in ch sp, ch 3, 1 dtr in next sc, ch 3, [1 dc, cl2] in ch sp, 1 dc in next st, ch 1, sk cl2, 1 dc in each of next 15 sts, ch 1, sk 1 dc, 1 dc in next st, cl2 in ch sp, 1 dc in next st) twice, ch 5, sk [cl2, 1 dc], 1 sc in ch sp, 1 sc in dtr, 1 sc in ch sp, ch 5, sk [1 dc, cl2], 1 dc in next st, [cl2, 1 dc] in ch sp, ch 3, 1 dtr in next sc, ch 3, [1 dc, cl2] in ch sp, 1 dc in next st, (ch 1, sk 1 st, 1 dc in next st) five times, 1 dc in each of last 2 dc.

ROW 11

1 dc in each of first 3 sts, (ch 1, sk ch 1, 1 dc in next st) six times, [cl2, 1 dc] in ch sp, ch 1, sk dtr, [1 dc, cl2] in ch sp, 1 dc in next st, (ch 6, sk [cl2, 1 dc], 1 sc in ch sp, 1 sc in each of middle 3 sc, 1 sc in ch sp, ch 6, sk [1 dc, cl2], 1 dc in next st, cl2 in ch sp, 1 dc in next st, ch 1, sk 1 dc, 1 dc in each of next 15 sts, ch 1, sk cl2, 1 dc in next st, [cl2, 1 dc] in ch sp, ch 1, sk dtr, [1 dc, cl2] in ch sp, 1 dc in next st) twice, ch 6, sk [cl2, 1 dc], 1 sc in ch sp, 1 sc in each of middle 3 sc, 1 sc in ch sp, ch 6, sk [1 dc, cl2], 1 dc in next st, cl2 in ch sp, 1 dc in next st, (ch 1, sk 1 st, 1 dc in next st) nine times, [cl2, 1 dc] in ch sp, ch 1, sk dtr, [1 dc, cl2] in ch sp, 1 dc in next st, (ch 1, sk 1 st, 1 dc in next st) nine times, cl2 in ch sp, 1 dc in next st, (ch 6, sk [cl2, 1 dc], 1 sc in ch sp, 1 sc in each of middle 3 sc, 1 sc in ch sp, ch 6, sk [1 dc, cl2], 1 dc in next st, [cl2, 1 dc] in ch sp, ch 1, sk dtr, [1 dc, cl2] in ch sp, 1 dc in next st, ch 1, sk cl2, 1 dc in each of next 15 sts, ch 1, sk 1 dc, 1 dc in next st, cl2 in ch sp, 1 dc in next st) twice, ch 6, sk [cl2, 1 dc], 1 sc in ch sp, 1 sc in each of middle 3 sc, 1 sc in ch sp, ch 6, sk [1 dc, cl2], 1 dc in next st, [cl2, 1 dc] in ch sp, ch 1, sk dtr, [1 dc, cl2] in ch sp, 1 dc in next st, (ch 1, sk 1 st, 1 dc in next st) six times, 1 dc in each of last 2 dc.

ROW 12

1 dc in each of first 3 sts, (ch 1, sk 1 st, 1 dc in next st) seven times, cl2 in ch sp, 1 dc in next st, (ch 7, sk [cl2, 1 dc], 1 sc in ch sp, 1 sc in each of middle 5 sc, 1 sc in ch sp, ch 7, sk [1 dc, cl2], 1 dc in next st, cl2 in ch sp, 1 dc in next st, ch 1, sk 1 dc, 1 dc in each of next 15 sts, ch 1, sk cl2, 1 dc in next st, cl2 in ch sp, 1 dc in next st) twice, ch 7, sk [cl2, 1 dc], 1 sc in ch sp, 1 sc in each of middle 5 sc, 1 sc in ch sp, ch 7, sk [1 dc, cl2], 1 dc in next st, cl2 in ch sp, 1 dc in next st, (ch 1, sk 1 st, 1 dc in next st) nine times, cl2 in ch sp, 1 dc in next st, (ch 1, sk 1 st, 1 dc in next st) nine times, cl2 in ch sp, 1 dc in next st, (ch 7, sk [cl2, 1 dc], 1 sc in ch sp, 1 sc in each of middle 5 sc, 1 sc in ch sp, ch 7, sk [1 dc, cl2], 1 dc in next st, cl2 in ch sp, 1 dc in next st, ch 1, sk cl2, 1 dc in each of next 15 sts, ch 1, sk 1 dc, 1 dc in next st, cl2 in ch sp, 1 dc in next st) twice, ch 7, sk [cl2, 1 dc], 1 sc in ch sp, 1 sc in each of middle 5 sc, 1 sc in ch sp, ch 7, sk [1 dc, cl2], 1 dc in next st, cl2 in ch sp, 1 dc in next st, (ch 1, sk 1 st, 1 dc in next st) seven times, 1 dc in each of last 2 dc.

ROW 13

1 dc in each of first 3 sts, (ch 1, sk ch 1, 1 dc in next st) eight times, [cl2, 1 dc] in ch sp, (ch 7, 1 sc in each of middle 5 sc, ch 7, [1 dc, cl2] in ch sp, 1 dc in next st, ch 1, sk cl2, 1 dc in next st, cl2 in ch sp, 1 dc in next st, ch 1, sk 1 dc, 1 dc in each of next 15 sts, ch 1, sk cl2, 1 dc in next st, [cl2, 1 dc] in ch sp) twice, ch 7, 1 sc in each of middle 5 sc, ch 7, [1 dc, cl2] in ch sp, 1 dc in next st, ch 1, sk cl2, 1 dc in next st, cl2 in ch sp, 1 dc in next st, (ch 1, sk 1 st, 1 dc in next st) seventeen times, cl2 in ch sp, 1 dc in next st, (ch 1, sk cl2, 1 dc in next st, [cl2, 1 dc] in ch sp, ch 7, 1 sc in each of middle 5 sc, ch 7, [1 dc, cl2] in ch sp, 1 dc in next st, ch 1, sk cl2, 1 dc in each of next 15 sts, ch 1, sk 1 dc, 1 dc in next st, cl2 in ch sp, 1 dc in next st) twice, ch 1, sk cl2, 1 dc in st, [cl2, 1 dc] in ch sp, ch 7, 1 sc in each of middle 5 sc, ch 7, [1 dc, cl2] in ch sp, 1 dc in next st, (ch 1, sk 1 st, 1 dc in next st) eight times, 1 dc in each of last 2 dc.

ROW 14

1 dc in each of first 3 sts, (ch 1, sk ch 1, 1 dc in next st) nine times, [cl2, 1 dc] in ch sp, (ch 5, 1 sc in each of middle 3 sc, ch 5, [1 dc, cl2] in ch sp, 1 dc in next st, ch 5, sk [cl2, 1 dc], 1 dtr in ch sp, ch 5, sk [1 dc, cl2], 1 dc in next st, cl2 in ch sp, 1 dc in next st, ch 1, sk 1 dc, 1 dc in each of next 15 sts, ch 1, sk cl2, 1 dc in next st, [cl2, 1 dc] in ch sp) twice, ch 5, 1 sc in each of middle 3 sc, ch 5, [1 dc, cl2] in ch sp, 1 dc in next st, ch 5, sk [cl2, 1 dc], 1 dtr in ch sp, ch 5, sk [1 dc, cl2], 1 dc in next st, cl2 in ch sp, 1 dc in next st, (ch 1, sk 1 st, 1 dc in next st) fifteen times, cl2 in ch sp, 1 dc in next st, (ch 5, sk [cl2, 1 dc], 1 dtr in ch sp, ch 5, sk [1 dc, cl2], 1 dc in next st, [cl2, 1 dc] in ch sp, ch 5, 1 sc in each of middle 3 sc, ch 5, [1 dc, cl2] in ch sp, 1 dc in next st, ch 1, sk cl2, 1 dc in each of next 15 sts, ch 1, sk 1 dc, 1 dc in next st, cl2 in ch sp, 1 dc in next st) twice, ch 5, sk [cl2, 1 dc], 1 dtr in ch sp, ch 5, sk [1 dc, cl2], 1 dc in next st, [cl2, 1 dc] in ch sp, ch 5, 1 sc in each of middle 3 sc, ch 5, [1 dc, cl2] in ch sp, 1 dc in next st, (ch 1, sk 1 st, 1 dc in next st) nine times, 1 dc in each of last 2 dc.

ROW 15

1 dc in each of first 3 sts, (ch 1, sk ch 1, 1 dc in next st) ten times, [cl2, 1 dc] in ch sp, (ch 3, 1 dtr in next sc, ch 3, [1 dc, cl2] in ch sp, 1 dc in next st, ch 5, sk [cl2, 1 dc], 1 sc in ch sp, 1 sc in dtr, 1 sc in ch sp, ch 5, sk [1 dc, cl2], 1 dc in next st, cl2 in ch sp, 1 dc in next st, ch 1, sk 1 dc, 1 dc in each of next 15 sts, ch 1, sk cl2, 1 dc in next st, [cl2, 1 dc] in ch sp) twice, ch 3, 1 dtr in next sc, ch 3, [1 dc, cl2] in ch sp, 1 dc in next st, ch 5, sk [cl2, 1 dc], 1 sc in ch sp, 1 sc in dtr, 1 sc in ch sp, ch 5, sk [1 dc, cl2], 1 dc in next st, cl2 in ch sp, 1 dc in next st, (ch 1, sk 1 st, 1 dc in next st) thirteen times, cl2 in ch sp, 1 dc in next st, (ch 5, sk [cl2, 1 dc], 1 sc in ch sp, 1 sc in dtr, 1 sc in ch sp, ch 5, sk [1 dc, cl2], 1 dc in next st, [cl2, 1 dc] in ch sp, ch 3, 1 dtr in next sc, ch 3, [1 dc, cl2] in ch sp, 1 dc in next st, ch 1, sk cl2, 1 dc in each of next 15 sts, ch 1, sk 1 dc, 1 dc in next st, cl2 in ch sp, 1 dc in next st) twice, ch 5, sk [cl2, 1 dc], 1 sc in ch sp, 1 sc in dtr, 1 sc in ch sp, ch 5, sk [1 dc, cl2], 1 dc in next st, [cl2, 1 dc] in ch sp, ch 3, 1 dtr in next sc, ch 3, [1 dc, cl2] in ch sp, 1 dc in next st, (ch 1, sk 1 st, 1 dc in next st) ten times, 1 dc in each of last 2 dc.

ROW 16

1 dc in each of first 3 sts, (ch 1, sk ch 1, 1 dc in next st) eleven times, [cl2, 1 dc] in ch sp, ch 1, sk dtr, [1 dc, cl2] in ch sp, 1 dc in next st, (ch 6, sk [cl2, 1 dc], 1 sc in ch sp, 1 sc in each of middle 3 sc, 1 sc in ch sp, ch 6, sk [1 dc, cl2], 1 dc in next st, cl2 in ch sp, 1 dc in next st, ch 1, sk 1 dc, 1 dc in each of next 15 sts, ch 1, sk cl2, 1 dc in next st, [cl2, 1 dc] in ch sp, ch 1, sk dtr, [1 dc, cl2] in ch sp, 1 dc in next st) twice, ch 6, sk [cl2, 1 dc], 1 sc in ch sp, 1 sc in each of middle 3 sc, 1 sc in ch sp, ch 6, sk [1 dc, cl2], 1 dc in next st, cl2 in ch sp, 1 dc in next st, (ch 1, sk 1 st, 1 dc in next st) eleven times, cl2 in ch sp, 1 dc in next st, (ch 6, sk [cl2, 1 dc], 1 sc in ch sp, 1 sc in each of middle 3 sc, 1 sc in ch sp, ch 6, sk [1 dc, cl2], 1 dc in next st, [cl2, 1 dc] in ch sp, ch 1, sk dtr, [1 dc, cl2] in ch sp, 1 dc in next st, ch 1, sk cl2, 1 dc in each of next 15 sts, ch 1, sk 1 dc, 1 dc in next st, cl2 in ch sp, 1 dc in next st) twice, ch 6, sk [cl2, 1 dc], 1 sc in ch sp, 1 sc in each of middle 3 sc, 1 sc in ch sp, ch 6, sk [1 dc, cl2], 1 dc in next st, [cl2, 1 dc] in ch sp, ch 1, sk dtr, [1 dc, cl2] in ch sp, 1 dc in next st, (ch 1, sk 1 st, 1 dc in next st) eleven times, 1 dc in each of last 2 dc.

ROW 17

1 dc in each of first 3 sts, (ch 1, sk 1 st, 1 dc in next st) twelve times, cl2 in ch sp, 1 dc in next st, (ch 7, sk [cl2, 1 dc], 1 sc in ch sp, 1 sc in each of middle 5 sc, 1 sc in ch sp, ch 7, sk [1 dc, cl2], 1 dc in next st, cl2 in ch sp, 1 dc in next st, ch 1, sk 1 dc, 1 dc in each of next 15 sts, ch 1, sk cl2, 1 dc in next st, cl2 in ch sp, 1 dc in next st) twice, ch 7, sk [cl2, 1 dc], 1 sc in ch sp, 1 sc in each of middle 5 sc, 1 sc in ch sp, ch 7, sk [1 dc, cl2], 1 dc in next st, cl2 in ch sp, 1 dc in next st, (ch 1, sk 1 st, 1 dc in next st) nine times, cl2 in ch sp, 1 dc in next st, (ch 7, sk [cl2, 1 dc], 1 sc in ch sp, 1 sc in each of middle 5 sc, 1 sc in ch sp, ch 7, sk [1 dc, cl2], 1 dc in next st, cl2 in ch sp, 1 dc in next st, ch 1, sk cl2, 1 dc in each of next 15 sts, ch 1, sk 1 dc, 1 dc in next st, cl2 in ch sp, 1 dc in next st) twice, ch 7, sk [cl2, 1 dc], 1 sc in ch sp, 1 sc in each of middle 5 sc, 1 sc in ch sp, ch 7, sk [1 dc, cl2], 1 dc in next st, cl2 in ch sp, 1 dc in next st, (ch 1, sk 1 st, 1 dc in next st) twelve times, 1 dc in each of last 2 dc.

ROW 18

1 dc in each of first 3 sts, (ch 1, sk ch 1, 1 dc in next st) thirteen times, [cl2, 1 dc] in ch sp, (ch 7, 1 sc in each of middle 5 sc, ch 7, [1 dc, cl2] in ch sp, 1 dc in next st, ch 1, sk cl2, 1 dc in next st, cl2 in ch sp, 1 dc in next st, ch 1, sk 1 dc, 1 dc in each of next 15 sts, ch 1, sk cl2, 1 dc in next st, [cl2, 1 dc] in ch sp) twice, ch 7, 1 sc in each of middle 5 sc, ch 7, [1 dc, cl2] in ch sp, 1 dc in next st, ch 1, sk cl2, 1 dc in next st, cl2 in ch sp, 1 dc in next st, (ch 1, sk 1 st, 1 dc in next st) seven times, cl2 in ch sp, 1 dc in next st, (ch 1, sk cl2, 1 dc in next st, [cl2, 1 dc] in ch sp, ch 7, 1 sc in each of middle 5 sc, ch 7, [1 dc, cl2] in ch sp, 1 dc in next st, ch 1, sk cl2, 1 dc in each of next 15 sts, ch 1, sk 1 dc, 1 dc in next st, cl2 in ch sp, 1 dc in next st) twice, ch 1, sk cl2, 1 dc in next st, [cl2, 1 dc] in ch sp, ch 7, 1 sc in each of middle 5 sc, ch 7, [1 dc, cl2] in ch sp, 1 dc in next st, (ch 1, sk 1 st, 1 dc in next st) thirteen times, 1 dc in each of last 2 dc.

ROW 19

1 dc in each of first 3 sts, (ch 1, sk ch 1, 1 dc in next st) fourteen times, [cl2, 1 dc] in ch sp, (ch 5, 1 sc in each of middle 3 sc, ch 5, [1 dc, cl2] in ch sp, 1 dc in next st, ch 5, sk [cl2, 1 dc], 1 dtr in ch sp, ch 5, sk [1 dc, cl2], 1 dc in next st, cl2 in ch sp, 1 dc in next st, ch 1, sk 1 dc, 1 dc in each of next 15 sts, ch 1, sk cl2, 1 dc in next st, [cl2, dc] in ch sp) twice, ch 5, 1 sc in each of middle 3 sc, ch 5, [1 dc, cl2] in ch sp, 1 dc in next st, ch 5, sk [cl2, 1 dc], 1 dtr in ch sp, ch 5, sk [1 dc, cl2], 1 dc in next st, cl2 in ch sp, 1 dc in next st, (ch 1, sk 1 st, 1 dc in next st) five times, cl2 in ch sp, 1 dc in next st, (ch 5, sk [cl2, 1 dc], 1 dtr in ch sp, ch 5, sk [1 dc, cl2], 1 dc in next st, [cl2, 1 dc] in ch sp, ch 5, 1 sc in each of middle 3 sc, ch 5, [1 dc, cl2] in ch sp, 1 dc in next st, ch 1, sk cl2, 1 dc in each of next 15 sts, ch 1, sk 1 dc, 1 dc in next st, cl2 in ch sp, 1 dc in next st) twice, ch 5, sk [cl2, 1 dc], 1 dtr in ch sp, ch 5, sk [1 dc, cl2], 1 dc in next st, [cl2, 1 dc] in ch sp, ch 5, 1 sc in each of middle 3 sc, ch 5, [1 dc, cl2] in ch sp, 1 dc in next st, (ch 1, sk 1 st, 1 dc in next st) fourteen times, 1 dc in each of last 2 dc.

ROW 20

1 dc in each of first 3 sts, (ch 1, sk ch 1, 1 dc in next st) fifteen times, [cl2, 1 dc] in ch sp, (ch 3, 1 dtr in next sc, ch 3, [1 dc, cl2] in ch sp, 1 dc in next st, ch 5, sk [cl2, 1 dc], 1 sc in ch sp, 1 sc in dtr, 1 sc in ch sp, ch 5, sk [1 dc, cl2], 1 dc in next st, cl2 in ch sp, 1 dc in next st, ch 1, sk 1 dc, 1 dc in each of next 15 sts, ch 1, sk cl2, 1 dc in next st, [cl2, 1 dc] in ch sp) twice, ch 3, 1 dtr in next sc, ch 3, [1 dc, cl2] in ch sp, 1 dc in next st, ch 5, sk [cl2, 1 dc], 1 sc in ch sp, 1 sc in dtr, 1 sc in ch sp, ch 5, sk [1 dc, cl2], 1 dc in next st, cl2 in ch sp, 1 dc in next st, (ch 1, sk 1 st, 1 dc in next st) three times, cl2 in ch sp, 1 dc in next st, (ch 5, sk [cl2, 1 dc], 1 sc in ch sp, 1 sc in dtr, 1 sc in ch sp, ch 5, sk [1 dc, cl2], 1 dc in next st, [cl2, 1 dc] in ch sp, ch 3, 1 dtr in next sc, ch 3, [1 dc, cl2] in ch sp, 1 dc in next st, ch 1, sk cl2, 1 dc in each of next 15 sts, ch 1, sk 1 dc, 1 dc in next st, cl2 in ch sp, 1 dc in next st) twice, ch 5, sk [cl2, 1 dc], 1 sc in ch sp, 1 sc in dtr, 1 sc in ch sp, ch 5, sk [cl2, 1 dc], 1 dc in next st, [cl2, 1 dc] in ch sp, ch 3, 1 dtr in next sc, ch 3, [1 dc, cl2] in ch sp, 1 dc in next st, (ch 1, sk 1 st, 1 dc in next st) fifteen times, 1 dc in each of last 2 dc.

ROW 21

1 dc in each of first 3 sts, (ch 1, sk ch 1, 1 dc in next st) sixteen times, [cl2, 1 dc] in ch sp, ch 1, sk dtr, [1 dc, cl2] in ch sp, 1 dc in next st, (ch 6, sk [cl2, 1 dc], 1 sc in ch sp, 1 sc in each of middle 3 sc, 1 sc in ch sp, ch 6, sk [1 dc, cl2], 1 dc in next st, cl2 in ch sp, 1 dc in next st, ch 1, sk 1 dc, 1 dc in each of next 15 sts, ch 1, sk cl2, 1 dc in next st, [cl2, 1 dc] in ch sp, ch 1, sk dtr, [1 dc, cl2] in ch sp, 1 dc in next st) twice, ch 6, sk [cl2, 1 dc], 1 sc in ch sp, 1 sc in each of middle 3 sc, 1 sc in ch sp, ch 6, sk [1 dc, cl2], 1 dc in next st, cl2 in ch sp, 1 dc in next st, ch 1, sk 1 st, 1 dc in next st, cl2 in ch sp, 1 dc in next st, (ch 6, sk [cl2, 1 dc], 1 sc in ch sp, 1 sc in each of middle 3 sc, 1 sc in ch sp, ch 6, sk [1 dc, cl2], 1 dc in next st, [cl2, 1 dc] in ch sp, ch 1, sk dtr, [1 dc, cl2] in ch sp, 1 dc in next st, ch 1, sk cl2, 1 dc in each of next 15 sts, ch 1, sk 1 dc, 1 dc in next st, cl2 in ch sp, 1 dc in next st) twice, ch 6, sk [cl2, 1 dc], 1 sc in ch sp, 1 sc in each of middle 3 sc, 1 sc in ch sp, ch 6, sk [1 dc, cl2], 1 dc in next st, [cl2, 1 dc] in ch sp, ch 1, sk dtr, [1 dc, cl2] in ch sp, 1 dc in next st, (ch 1, sk 1 st, 1 dc in next st) sixteen times, 1 dc in each of last 2 dc.

⟶

ROW 22

1 dc in each of first 3 dc, (ch 1, sk 1 st, 1 dc in next st) seventeen times, cl2 in ch sp, 1 dc in next st, (ch 7, sk [cl2, 1 dc], 1 sc in ch sp, 1 sc in each of middle 5 sc, 1 sc in ch sp, ch 7, sk [1 dc, cl2], 1 dc in next st, cl2 in ch sp, 1 dc in next st, ch 1, sk 1 dc, 1 dc in each of next 15 sts, ch 1, sk cl2, 1 dc in next st, cl2 in ch sp, 1 dc in next st) twice, ch 7, sk [cl2, 1 dc], 1 sc in ch sp, 1 sc in each of middle 5 sc, 1 sc in ch sp, ch 7, sk [1 dc, cl2], 1 dc in next st, cl2 in ch sp, 1 dc in next st, (ch 7, sk [cl2, 1 dc], 1 sc in ch sp, 1 sc in each of middle 5 sc, 1 sc in ch sp, ch 7, sk [1 dc, cl2], 1 dc in next st, cl2 in ch sp, 1 dc in next st, ch 1, sk cl2, 1 dc in each of next 15 sts, ch 1, sk 1 dc, 1 dc in next st, cl2 in ch sp, 1 dc in next st) twice, ch 7, sk [cl2, 1 dc], 1 sc in ch sp, 1 sc in each of middle 5 sc, 1 sc in ch sp, ch 7, sk [1 dc, cl2], 1 dc in next st, cl2 in ch sp, 1 dc in next st, (ch 1, sk 1 st, 1 dc in next st) seventeen times, 1 dc in each of last 2 dc.

ROW 23

1 dc in each of first 3 sts, (ch 1, sk ch 1, 1 dc in next st) sixteen times, cl2 in ch sp, 1 dc in next st, ch 1, sk cl2, 1 dc in next st, [cl2, 1 dc] in ch sp, (ch 7, 1 sc in each of middle 5 sc, ch 7, [1 dc, cl2] in ch sp, 1 dc in next st, ch 1, sk cl2, 1 dc in each of next 15 sts, ch 1, sk 1 dc, 1 dc in next st, cl2 in ch sp, 1 dc in next st, ch 1, sk cl2, 1 dc in next st, [cl2, 1 dc] in ch sp) twice, ch 7, 1 sc in each of middle 5 sc, ch 7, [1 dc, cl2] in ch sp, 1 dc in next st, ch 1, sk cl2, 1 dc in next st, [cl2, 1 dc] in ch sp, (ch 7, 1 sc in each of middle 5 sc, ch 7, [1 dc, cl2] in ch sp, 1 dc in next st, ch 1, sk cl2, 1 dc in next st, cl2 in ch sp, 1 dc in next st, ch 1, sk 1 st, 1 dc in each of next 15 sts, ch 1, sk cl2, 1 dc in next st, [cl2, 1 dc] in ch sp) twice, ch 7, 1 sc in each of middle 5 sc, ch 7, [1 dc, cl2] in ch sp, 1 dc in next st, ch 1, sk cl2, 1 dc in next st, cl2 in ch sp, 1 dc in next st, (ch 1, sk 1 st, 1 dc in next st) sixteen times, 1 dc in each of last 2 dc.

ROW 24

1 dc in each of first 3 sts, (ch 1, sk ch 1, 1 dc in next st) fifteen times, cl2 in ch sp, 1 dc in next st, (ch 5, sk [cl2, 1 dc], 1 dtr in ch sp, ch 5, sk [1 dc, cl2], 1 dc in next st, [cl2, 1 dc] in ch sp, ch 5, 1 sc in each of middle 3 sc, ch 5, [1 dc, cl2] in ch sp, 1 dc in next st, ch 1, sk cl2, 1 dc in each of next 15 sts, ch 1, sk 1 dc, 1 dc in next st, cl2 in ch sp, 1 dc in next st) twice, ch 5, sk [cl2, 1 dc], 1 dtr in ch sp, ch 5, sk [1 dc, cl2], 1 dc in next st, [cl2, 1 dc] in ch sp, ch 5, 1 sc in each of middle 3 sc, ch 5, [1 dc, cl2] in ch sp, 1 dc in next st, (ch 1, sk 1 st, 1 dc in next st) three times, [cl2, 1 dc] in ch sp, (ch 5, 1 sc in each of middle 3 sc, ch 5, [1 dc, cl2] in ch sp, 1 dc in next st, ch 5, sk [cl2, 1 dc], 1 dtr in ch sp, ch 5, sk [1 dc, cl2], 1 dc in next st, cl2 in ch sp, 1 dc in next st, ch 1, sk 1 dc, 1 dc in each of next 15 sts, ch 1, sk cl2, 1 dc in next st, [cl2, 1 dc] in ch sp) twice, ch 5, 1 sc in each of middle 3 sc, ch 5, [1 dc, cl2] in ch sp, 1 dc in next st, ch 5, sk [cl2, 1 dc], 1 dtr in ch sp, ch 5, sk [1 dc, cl2], 1 dc in next st, cl2 in ch sp, 1 dc in next st, (ch 1, sk 1 st, 1 dc in next st) fifteen times, 1 dc in each of last 2 dc.

ROW 25

1 dc in each of first 3 sts, (ch 1, sk ch 1, 1 dc in next st) fourteen times, cl2 in ch sp, 1 dc in next st, (ch 5, sk [cl2, 1 dc], 1 sc in ch sp, 1 sc in dtr, 1 sc in ch sp, ch 5, sk [1 dc, cl2], 1 dc in next st, [cl2, 1 dc] in ch sp, ch 3, 1 dtr in next sc, ch 3, [1 dc, cl2] in ch sp, 1 dc in next st, ch 1, sk cl2, 1 dc in each of next 15 sts, ch 1, sk 1 dc, 1 dc in next st, cl2 in ch sp, 1 dc in next st) twice, ch 5, sk [cl2, 1 dc], 1 sc in ch sp, 1 sc in dtr, 1 sc in ch sp, ch 5, sk [1 dc, cl2], 1 dc in next st, [cl2, 1 dc] in ch sp, ch 3, 1 dtr in next sc, ch 3, [1 dc, cl2] in ch sp, 1 dc in next st, (ch 1, sk 1 st, 1 dc in next st) five times, [cl2, 1 dc] in ch sp, (ch 3, 1 dtr in next sc, ch 3, [1 dc, cl2] in ch sp, 1 dc in next st, ch 5, sk [cl2, 1 dc], 1 sc in ch sp, 1 sc in dtr, 1 sc in ch sp, ch 5, sk [1 dc, cl2], 1 dc in next st, cl2 in ch sp, 1 dc in next st, ch 1, sk 1 dc, 1 dc in each of next 15 sts, ch 1, sk cl2, 1 dc in next st, [cl2, 1 dc] in ch sp) twice, ch 3, 1 dtr in next sc, ch 3, [1 dc, cl2] in ch sp, 1 dc in next st, ch 5, sk [cl2, 1 dc], 1 sc in ch sp, 1 sc in dtr, 1 sc in ch sp, ch 5, sk [1 dc, cl2], 1 dc in next st, cl2 in ch sp, 1 dc in next st, (ch 1, sk 1 st, 1 dc in next st) fourteen times, 1 dc in each of last 2 dc.

ROW 26

1 dc in each of first 3 sts, (ch 1, sk ch 1, 1 dc in next st) thirteen times, cl2 in ch sp, 1 dc in next st, (ch 6, sk [cl2, 1 dc], 1 sc in ch sp, 1 sc in each of middle 3 sc, 1 sc in ch sp, ch 6, sk [1 dc, cl2], 1 dc in next st, [cl2, 1 dc] in ch sp, ch 1, sk dtr, [1 dc, cl2] in ch sp, 1 dc in next st, ch 1, sk cl2, 1 dc in each of next 15 sts, ch 1, sk 1 dc, 1 dc in next st, cl2 in ch sp, 1 dc in next st) twice, ch 6, sk [cl2, 1 dc], 1 sc in ch sp, 1 sc in each of middle 3 sc, 1 sc in ch sp, ch 6, sk [1 dc, cl2], 1 dc in next st, [cl2, 1 dc] in ch sp, ch 1, sk dtr, [1 dc, cl2] in ch sp, 1 dc in next st, (ch 1, sk 1 st, 1 dc in next st) seven times, [cl2, 1 dc] in ch sp, (ch 1, sk dtr, [1 dc, cl2] in ch sp, 1 dc in next st, ch 6, sk [cl2, 1 dc], 1 sc in ch sp, 1 sc in each of middle 3 sc, 1 sc in ch sp, ch 6, sk [1 dc, cl2], 1 dc in next st, cl2 in ch sp, 1 dc in next st, ch 1, sk 1 dc, 1 dc in each of next 15 sts, ch 1, sk cl2, 1 dc in next st, [cl2, 1 dc] in ch sp) twice, ch 1, sk dtr, [1 dc, cl2] in ch sp, 1 dc in next st, ch 6, sk [cl2, 1 dc], 1 sc in ch sp, 1 sc in each of middle 3 sc, 1 sc in ch sp, ch 6, sk [1 dc, cl2], 1 dc in next st, cl2 in ch sp, 1 dc in next st, (ch 1, sk 1 st, 1 dc in next st) thirteen times, 1 dc in each of last 2 dc.

ROW 27

1 dc in each of first 3 sts, (ch 1, sk ch 1, 1 dc in next st) twelve times, cl2 in ch sp, 1 dc in next st, (ch 7, sk [cl2, 1 dc], 1 sc in ch sp, 1 sc in each of middle 5 sc, 1 sc in ch sp, ch 7, sk [1 dc, cl2], 1 dc in next st, cl2 in ch sp, 1 dc in next st, ch 1, sk cl2, 1 dc in each of next 15 sts, ch 1, sk 1 dc, 1 dc in next st, cl2 in ch sp, 1 dc in next st) twice, ch 7, sk [cl2, 1 dc], 1 sc in ch sp, 1 sc in each of middle 5 sc, 1 sc in ch sp, ch 7, sk [1 dc, cl2], 1 dc in next st, cl2 in ch sp, 1 dc in next st, (ch 1, sk 1 st, 1 dc in next st) nine times, cl2 in ch sp, 1 dc in next st, (ch 7, sk [cl2, 1 dc], 1 sc in ch sp, 1 sc in each of middle 5 sc, 1 sc in ch sp, ch 7, sk [1 dc, cl2], 1 dc in next st, cl2 in ch sp, 1 dc in next st, ch 1, sk 1 dc, 1 dc in each of next 15 sts, ch 1, sk cl2, 1 dc in next st, cl2 in ch sp, 1 dc in next st) twice, ch 7, sk [cl2, 1 dc], 1 sc in ch sp, 1 sc in each of middle 5 sc, 1 sc in ch sp, ch 7, sk [1 dc, cl2], 1 dc in next st, cl2 in ch sp, 1 dc in next st, (ch 1, sk 1 st, 1 dc in next st) twelve times, 1 dc in each of last 2 dc.

ROW 28

1 dc in each of first 3 sts, (ch 1, sk ch 1, 1 dc in next st) eleven times, cl2 in ch sp, 1 dc in next st, ch 1, sk cl2, 1 dc in next st, [cl2, 1 dc] in ch sp, (ch 7, 1 sc in each of middle 5 sc, ch 7, [1 dc, cl2] in ch sp, 1 dc in next st, ch 1, sk cl2, 1 dc in each of next 15 sts, ch 1, sk 1 dc, 1 dc in next st, cl2 in ch sp, 1 dc in next st, ch 1, sk cl2, 1 dc in next st, [cl2, 1 dc] in ch sp) twice, ch 7, 1 sc in each of middle 5 sc, ch 7, [1 dc, cl2] in ch sp, 1 dc in next st, (ch 1, sk 1 st, 1 dc in next st) eleven times, [cl2, 1 dc] in ch sp, (ch 7, 1 sc in each of middle 5 sc, ch 7, [1 dc, cl2] in ch sp, 1 dc in next st, ch 1, sk cl2, 1 dc in next st, cl2 in ch sp, 1 dc in next st, ch 1, sk 1 dc, 1 dc in each of next 15 sts, ch 1, sk cl2, 1 dc in next st, [cl2, 1 dc] in ch sp) twice, ch 7, 1 sc in each of middle 5 sc, ch 7, [1 dc, cl2] in ch sp, 1 dc in next st, ch 1, sk cl2, 1 dc in next st, cl2 in ch sp, 1 dc in next st, (ch 1, sk 1 st, 1 dc in next st) eleven times, 1 dc in each of last 2 dc.

→

ROW 29

1 dc in each of first 3 sts, (ch 1, sk ch 1, 1 dc in next st) ten times, cl2 in ch sp, 1 dc in next st, (ch 5, sk [cl2, 1 dc], 1 dtr in ch sp, ch 5, sk [1 dc, cl2], 1 dc in next st, [cl2, 1 dc] in ch sp, ch 5, 1 sc in each of middle 3 sc, ch 5, [1 dc, cl2] in ch sp, 1 dc in next st, ch 1, sk cl2, 1 dc in each of next 15 sts, ch 1, sk 1 dc, 1 dc in next st, cl2 in ch sp, 1 dc in next st) twice, ch 5, sk [cl2, 1 dc], 1 dtr in ch sp, ch 5, sk [1 dc, cl2], 1 dc in next st, [cl2, 1 dc] in ch sp, ch 5, 1 sc in each of middle 3 sc, ch 5, [1 dc, cl2] in ch sp, 1 dc in next st, (ch 1, sk 1 st, 1 dc in next st) thirteen times, [cl2, 1 dc] in ch sp, (ch 5, 1 sc in each of middle 3 sc, ch 5, [1 dc, cl2] in ch sp, 1 dc in next st, ch 5, sk [cl2, 1 dc], 1 dtr in ch sp, ch 5, sk [1 dc, cl2], 1 dc in next st, cl2 in ch sp, 1 dc in next st, ch 1, sk 1 dc, 1 dc in each of next 15 sts, ch 1, sk cl2, 1 dc in next st, [cl2, 1 dc] in ch sp) twice, ch 5, 1 sc in each of middle 3 sc, ch 5, [1 dc, cl2] in ch sp, 1 dc in next st, ch 5, sk [cl2, 1 dc], 1 dtr in ch sp, ch 5, sk [1 dc, cl2], 1 dc in next st, cl2 in ch sp, 1 dc in next st, (ch 1, sk 1 st, 1 dc in next st) ten times, 1 dc in each of last 2 dc.

ROW 30

1 dc in each of first 3 sts, (ch 1, sk ch 1, 1 dc in next st) nine times, cl2 in ch sp, 1 dc in next st, (ch 5, sk [cl2, 1 dc], 1 sc in ch sp, 1 sc in dtr, 1 sc in ch sp, ch 5, sk [1 dc, cl2], 1 dc in next st, [cl2, 1 dc] in ch sp, ch 3, 1 dtr in next sc, ch 3, [1 dc, cl2] in ch sp, 1 dc in next st, ch 1, sk cl2, 1 dc in each of next 15 sts, ch 1, sk 1 dc, 1 dc in next st, cl2 in ch sp, 1 dc in next st) twice, ch 5, sk [cl2, 1 dc], 1 sc in ch sp, 1 sc in dtr, 1 sc in ch sp, ch 5, sk [1 dc, cl2], 1 dc in next st, [cl2, 1 dc] in ch sp, ch 3, 1 dtr in next sc, ch 3, [1 dc, cl2] in ch sp, 1 dc in next st, (ch 1, sk 1 st, 1 dc in next st) fifteen times, [cl2, 1 dc] in ch sp, (ch 3, 1 dtr in next sc, ch 3, [1 dc, cl2] in ch sp, 1 dc in next st, ch 5, sk [cl2, 1 dc], 1 sc in ch sp, 1 sc in dtr, 1 sc in ch sp, ch 5, sk [1 dc, cl2], 1 dc in next st, cl2 in ch sp, 1 dc in next st, ch 1, sk 1 dc, 1 dc in each of next 15 sts, ch 1, sk cl2, 1 dc in next st, [cl2, 1 dc] in ch sp) twice, ch 3, 1 dtr in next sc, ch 3, [1 dc, cl2] in ch sp, 1 dc in next st, ch 5, sk [cl2, 1 dc], 1 sc in ch sp, 1 sc in dtr, 1 sc in ch sp, ch 5, sk [1 dc, cl2], 1 dc in next st, cl2 in ch sp, 1 dc in next st, (ch 1, sk 1 st, 1 dc in next st) nine times, 1 dc in each of last 2 dc.

ROW 31

1 dc in each of first 3 sts, (ch 1, sk ch 1, 1 dc in next st) eight times, cl2 in ch sp, 1 dc in next st, (ch 6, sk [cl2, 1 dc], 1 sc in ch sp, 1 sc in each of middle 3 sc, 1 sc in ch sp, ch 6, sk [1 dc, cl2], 1 dc in next st, [cl2, 1 dc] in ch sp, ch 1, sk dtr, [1 dc, cl2] in ch sp, 1 dc in next st, ch 1, sk cl2, 1 dc in each of next 15 sts, ch 1, sk 1 dc, 1 dc in next st, cl2 in ch sp, 1 dc in next st) twice, ch 6, sk [cl2, 1 dc], 1 sc in ch sp, 1 sc in each of middle 3 sc, 1 sc in ch sp, ch 6, sk [1 dc, cl2], 1 dc in next st, [cl2, 1 dc] in ch sp, ch 1, sk dtr, [1 dc, cl2] in ch sp, 1 dc in next st, (ch 1, sk 1 st, 1 dc in next st) seventeen times, [cl2, 1 dc] in ch sp, (ch 1, sk dtr, [1 dc, cl2] in ch sp, 1 dc in next st, ch 6, sk [cl2, 1 dc], 1 sc in ch sp, 1 sc in each of middle 3 sc, 1 sc in ch sp, ch 6, sk [1 dc, cl2], 1 dc in next st, cl2 in ch sp, 1 dc in next st, ch 1, sk 1 dc, 1 dc in each of next 15 sts, ch 1, sk cl2, 1 dc in next st, [cl2, 1 dc] in ch sp) twice, ch 1, sk dtr, [1 dc, cl2] in ch sp, 1 dc in next st, ch 6, sk [cl2, 1 dc], 1 sc in ch sp, 1 sc in each of middle 3 sc, 1 sc in ch sp, ch 6, sk [1 dc, cl2], 1 dc in next st, cl2 in ch sp, 1 dc in next st, (ch 1, sk 1 st, 1 dc in next st) eight times, 1 dc in each of last 2 dc.

ROW 32

1 dc in each of first 3 sts, (ch 1, sk 1 st, 1 dc in next st) seven times, cl2 in ch sp, 1 dc in next st, (ch 7, sk [cl2, 1 dc], 1 sc in ch sp, 1 sc in each of middle 5 sc, 1 sc in ch sp, ch 7, sk [1 dc, cl2], 1 dc in next st, cl2 in ch sp, 1 dc in next st, ch 1, sk cl2, 1 dc in each of next 15 sts, ch 1, sk 1 dc, 1 dc in next st, cl2 in ch sp, 1 dc in next st) twice, ch 7, sk [cl2, 1 dc], 1 sc in ch sp, 1 sc in each of next 5 sts, 1 sc in ch sp, ch 7, sk [1 dc, cl2], 1 dc in next st, cl2 in ch sp, 1 dc in next st, (ch 1, sk 1 st, 1 dc in next st) nine times, cl2 in ch sp, 1 dc in next st, (ch 1, sk 1 st, 1 dc in next st) nine times, cl2 in ch sp, 1 dc in next st, (ch 7, sk [cl2, 1 dc], 1 sc in ch sp, 1 sc in each of middle 5 sc, 1 sc in ch sp, ch 7, sk [1 dc, cl2], 1 dc in next st, cl2 in ch sp, 1 dc in next st, ch 1, sk 1 dc, 1 dc in each of next 15 sts, ch 1, sk cl2, 1 dc in next st, cl2 in ch sp, 1 dc in next st) twice, ch 7, sk [cl2, 1 dc], 1 sc in ch sp, 1 sc in each of middle 5 sc, 1 sc in ch sp, ch 7, sk [1 dc, cl2], 1 dc in next st, cl2 in ch sp, 1 dc in next st, (ch 1, sk 1 st, 1 dc in next st) seven times, 1 dc in each of last 2 dc.

Rep rows 3–32 until the work measures the correct length. Instead of working row 32, work the final row 32 as follows:

FINAL ROW 32

1 dc in each of first 3 sts, (ch 1, sk 1 st, 1 dc in next st) seven times, cl2 in ch sp, 1 dc in next st, (ch 7, sk [cl2, 1 dc], sc2tog in ch sp and first sc (of group of 5), 1 sc in each of next 3 sts, sc2tog over fifth sc (of group of 5) and in ch sp, ch 7, sk [1 dc, cl2], 1 dc in next st, cl2 in ch sp, 1 dc in next st, ch 1, sk cl2, 1 dc in each of next 15 sts, ch 1, sk 1 dc, 1 dc in next st, cl2 in ch sp, 1 dc in next st) twice, ch 7, sk [cl2, 1 dc], sc2tog in ch sp and first sc (of group of 5), 1 sc in each of next 3 sts, sc2tog over fifth sc (of group of 5) and in ch sp, ch 7, sk [1 dc, cl2], 1 dc in next st, cl2 in ch sp, 1 dc in next st, (ch 1, sk 1 st, 1 dc in next st) nine times, cl2 in ch sp, 1 dc in next st, (ch 1, sk 1 st, 1 dc in next st) nine times, cl2 in ch sp, 1 dc in next st, (ch 7, sk [cl2, 1 dc], sc2tog in ch sp and first sc (of group of 5), 1 sc in each of next 3 sts, sc2tog over fifth sc (of group of 5) and in ch sp, ch 7, sk [1 dc, cl2], 1 dc in next st, cl2 in ch sp, 1 dc in next st, ch 1, sk 1 dc, 1 dc in each of next 15 sts, ch 1, sk cl2, 1 dc in next st, cl2 in ch sp, 1 dc in next st) twice, ch 7, sk [cl2, 1 dc], sc2tog in ch sp and first sc (of group of 5), 1 sc in each of next 3 sts, sc2tog over fifth sc (of group of 5) and in ch sp, ch 7, sk [1 dc, cl2], 1 dc in next st, cl2 in ch sp, 1 dc in next st, (ch 1, sk 1 st, 1 dc in next st) seven times, 1 dc in each of last 2 dc.

LAST ROW

1 dc in each st and 6 dc in each loop of 7 chains (275 sts).

Fasten off and weave in the ends.

Chart A
(covers stitches 1–98)
Red rows indicate repeat

Chart B
(covers stitches 99–178)
Red rows indicate repeat

Chart C
(covers stitches 179–275)
Red rows indicate repeat

Colour Splendour

By working multiple long, narrow strips, this pattern provides a true splash of colour. It's easy to crochet, and before you know it, you will have a splendid, multicoloured blanket.

MATERIALS

24 balls of **Durable Comfy 5-ply (sport) microfibre acrylic yarn** (100g/3½oz/266m/291yd) in the following colours:

- 3 balls of Deep Fuchsia/dark pink (238) (A)
- 3 balls of Pink Lemonade/hot pink (242) (B)
- 3 balls of Light Pink (203) (C)
- 3 balls of Bright Mint (2136) (D)
- 3 balls of Atlantis/teal (342) (E)
- 3 balls of Cyan Blue (373) (F)
- 2 balls of Petrol/dark blue (375) (G)
- 4 balls of White (310) (H)

TOOLS

3.5mm (US E-4, UK 9/10) crochet hook

Stitch markers

FINISHED SIZE

150 × 210cm (59 × 83in)

DIFFICULTY LEVEL

Medium

KEY

– long tail foundation

– chain

– slip stitch

– single crochet

– double crochet

– double crochet 3 stitches together

PATTERN NOTES

The blanket is worked in rows, and you will need to turn the work at the end of each row. This is not in the written instructions.

Start with the strip on the right-hand side in yarn A then work and attach the strip in yarn B to the left of this, continue in this way working strips in yarns C, D, E, F, G then work strips in yarns F, E, D, C, B, A.

The strips are joined together whilst working round 14.

The first st in each round is created by working x ch, depending on the st that it replaces (e.g. dc = 3 ch). This is not in the written instructions.

STITCHES AND ABBREVIATIONS USED

ch	chain(s)
ch sp(s)	chain space(s)
dc	double crochet
dc3tog	double crochet the next 3 stitches together
PM	place marker
RS	right side
sc	single crochet
sk	skip
sl st	slip stitch
st(s)	stitch(es)
WS	wrong side

ADDITIONAL STITCHES

DOUBLE CROCHET 3 TOGETHER (DC3TOG)

*Yarn over, insert hook into next stitch, yarn over and pull through, yarn over and pull through two loops on hook, rep from * in the next 2 stitches (four loops on hook), yarn over and pull through all loops on hook.

STRIP

Make 389 sts using the long tail foundation method.

ROW 1 (RS)
1 dc in each st (389 sts).

ROW 2 (WS)
1 dc in each of first 3 sts, *1 dc in next st, ch 1, sk 1 st, rep from * to last 4 sts, 1 dc in each of last 4 sts.

ROW 3
1 dc in each st.

ROW 4
1 sc in each st.

ROW 5
1 dc in each of first 3 sts, ch 1, *dc3tog, ch 5, sk 1 st, rep from * to last 6 sts, dc3tog, ch 1, 1 dc in each of last 3 sts.

ROW 6
1 dc in each of first 3 sts, *ch 5, 1 sc in 5-ch sp*, rep from * in each 5-ch sp, ch 5, 1 dc in each of last 3 sts.

ROW 7
1 dc in each of first 3 sts, 3 dc in middle ch of first 5-ch sp, *ch 1, 3 dc in middle ch of next 5-ch sp, rep from * to last 3 sts, 1 dc in each of last 3 sts.

ROW 8
1 sc in each dc and ch.

ROW 9
1 dc in each st.

ROW 10
1 dc in each of first 3 sts, *1 dc in next st, ch 1, sk 1 st, rep from * to last 4 sts, 1 dc in each of last 4 sts.

ROW 11
1 dc in each ch and dc.

ROW 12
1 sc in each st.

Fasten off and weave in ends.

With RS facing, now work in rounds using yarn H around the strip.

ROUND 13
Join yarn H in last st worked in row 12, 1 sc in same st, 1 sc in each st to last st on this side, 3 sc in last st (PM in centre of these 3 sts), turn to work along left short side.

Work 19 sc evenly along the short side, turn to work along foundation sts, 3 sc in first foundation st (PM in centre of these 3 sts), 1 sc in each foundation st to the last st, 3 sc in last foundation st (PM in centre of these 3 sts).

Rotate to work along right short side, work 19 sc evenly along the short side, 2 dc in same st as beginning sc (PM in second of these 2 sts), join with a sl st.

NOTE
Round 14 should only be worked for the first strip. For each subsequent strip work round 14A to join to the previous strip.

ROUND 14
1 sc in first sc, *ch 5, sk 3 sc, 1 sc in next sc, rep from * to marked st, 3 sc in marked st (PM in centre of these 3 sts).

Rotate to work along left short side, 1 sc in first sc, (ch 5, sk 3 sc, 1 sc in next sc) five times, 3 sc in marked st (PM in centre of these 3 sts).

Rotate to work along bottom long side, 1 sc in first sc, *ch 5, sk 3 sc, 1 sc in next sc, rep from * to marked st, 3 sc in marked st (PM in centre of these 3 sts),

Turn to work along right short side, 1 sc in first sc, (ch 5, sk 3 sc, 1 sc in next sc) five times, 3 sc in marked st (PM in centre of these 3 sts), join with a sl st.

Fasten off and weave in ends.

JOINING

ROUND 14A
1 sc in first sc, *ch 5, sk 3 sc, 1 sc in next sc, rep from * to marked st, 3 sc in marked st (PM in centre of these 3 sts).

Rotate to work along left short side, 1 sc in first sc, (ch 5, sk 3 sc, 1 sc in next sc) five times, 3 sc in marked st (PM in centre of these 3 sts),

Rotate to work along bottom long side, positioning the strips together with RS facing upwards and strip 1 above strip 2, 1 sc in first sc, ch 2, 1 sc in first 5-ch sp of previous strip, ch 2, sk 3 sc, 1 sc in next sc, *ch 2, 1 sc in next 5-ch sp of previous strip, ch 2, sk 3 sc, 1 sc in next sc, rep from * to marked st, 3 sc in marked st (PM in centre of these 3 sts),

Rotate to work along right short side 1 sc in first sc, (ch 5, sk 3 sc, 1 sc in next sc) five times, 3 sc in marked st (PM in centre of these 3 sts), join with a sl st.

Fasten off and weave in ends.

Keep all markers attached as they are needed when working the border.

Work the remaining 11 strips in the same way using the colours in the order given above.

Chart A
Cross section of Round 14a

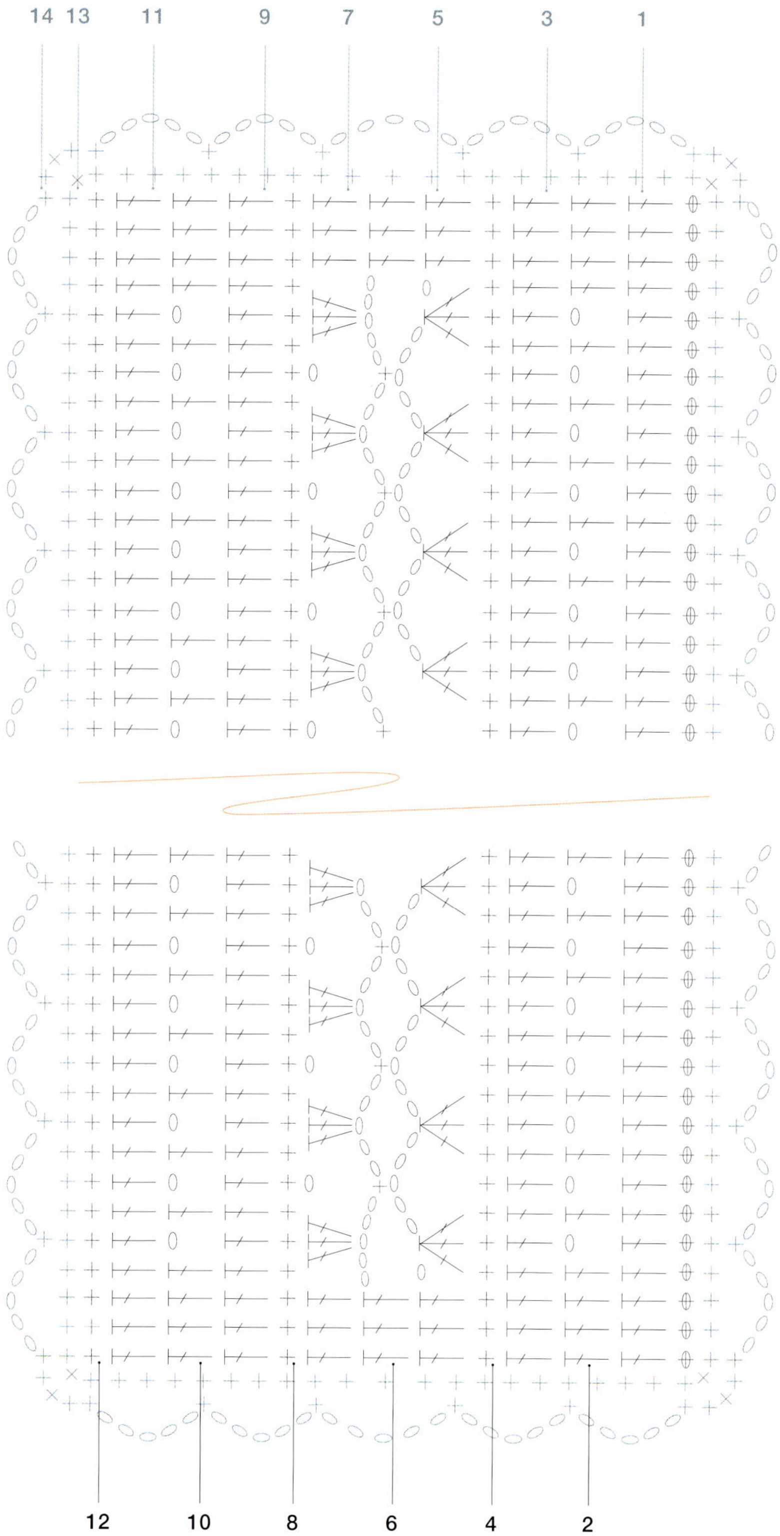

Chart B
Strip pattern

Chart C
Border

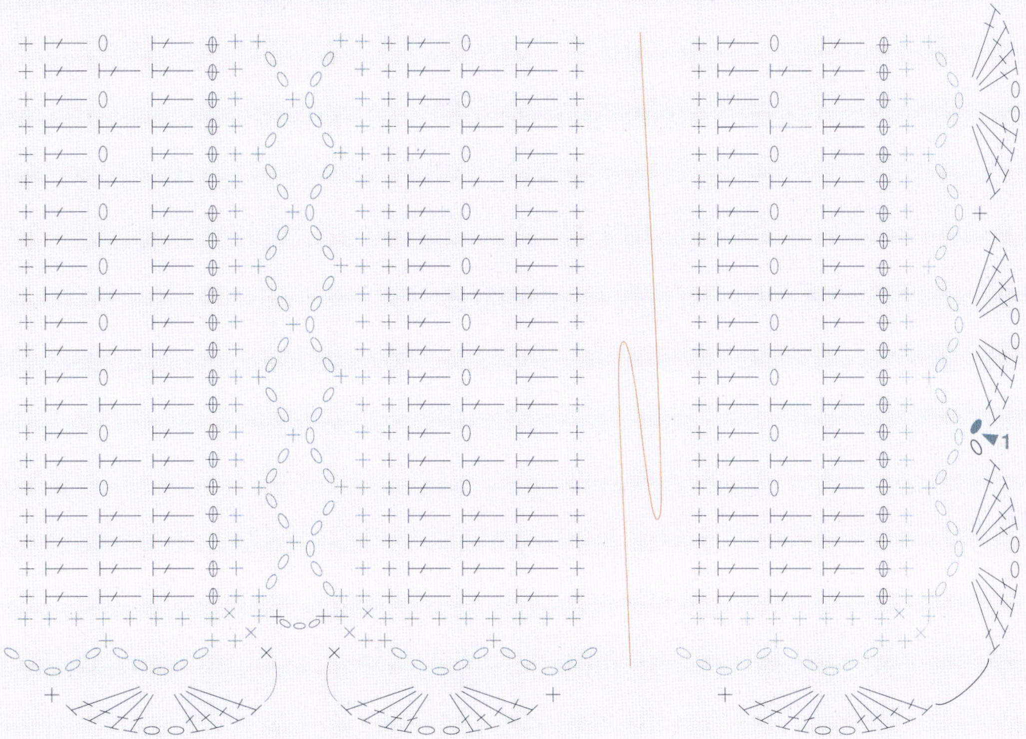

BORDER

ROUND 1

With RS facing, join yarn H with a sl st in the second 5-ch sp of a long side, *[4 dc, ch 2, 4 dc] in next 5-ch sp, 1 sc in next 5-ch sp, rep from * to last 5-ch sp of this side, [4 dc, ch 2, 4 dc] in last 5-ch sp.

Rotate to work along short side of all strips: *([4 dc, ch 2, 4 dc] in next 5-ch sp, 1 sc in next 5-ch sp) twice, [4 dc, ch 2, 4 dc] in next 5-ch sp, sk 2 sc, 1 sc in marked st, 1 sc in next sc, ch 3, move to following strip, 1 sc in st before marked st, 1 sc in marked st, sk 2 sc, rep from * along all strips, on the last strip work [4 dc, ch 2, 4 dc] in last 5-ch sp.

Work the next long side and the next short side in the same way, then work [4 dc, ch 2, 4 dc] in the first 5-ch sp of the first long side, ch 1, join with a sl st.

Fasten off and weave in ends.

Cozy Warmth

A lovely warm blanket, perfect for snuggling on the sofa.

The squares that form this blanket are worked in different stitch patterns, just like a sampler.

MATERIALS

38 balls of **Durable Cosy Fine DK (8-ply/light worsted) 58% cotton, 42% acrylic yarn** (50g/1¾oz/105m/115yd) in the following colours:

- 4 balls of Vintage Pink/dusky pink (225) (A)
- 7 balls of Blue Grey (289) (B)
- 18 balls of Silver Grey (2228) (C)
- 9 balls of Vintage Green (2134) (D)

TOOLS

4mm (US G-6, UK 8), 3.5mm (US E-4, UK 9/10) and 5mm (US H-8, UK 6) crochet hooks

Tapestry needle

Stitch markers

FINISHED SIZE

1 square
21.5 × 21.5cm (8½ × 8½in)

Blanket
115 × 160cm (45 × 63in)

DIFFICULTY LEVEL

Medium

KEY

 *– long tail foundation*

 *– chain*

 *– single crochet*

 *– double crochet*

 *– cluster A*

 *– cluster B*

 *– cluster C*

 *– cluster D*

PATTERN NOTES

The squares are worked in rows, which means you will need to turn the work at the end of each row.

To achieve the same size square, you may need to change hook sizes, depending on your tension.˙Work a square in pattern 1 and use it as a gauge for the rest of the squares.

The first st in each round is created by working × ch, depending on the st that it replaces (e.g. dc = 3 ch). This is not in the written instructions.

STITCHES AND ABBREVIATIONS USED

blo	back loop only
ch	chain(s)
ch sp(s)	chain space(s)
dc	double crochet
FPdtr2tog	front post double treble 2 together
PM	place marker
RS	right side
sc	single crochet
sk	skip
sl st	slip stitch
st(s)	stitch(es)
tog	together
WS	wrong side

SPECIAL STITCHES

clA (cluster A) FPdtr2tog in st 2 rows below next st.

clB (cluster B) see images on page 65; insert hook in st indicated, pull up a loop (photo 1), insert in sc 1 row below (photo 2), pull up a loop (photo 3), insert in sc 2 rounds below (photo 4), pull up a loop (photo 5), yarn over (photo 6), pull through all loops (photo 7).

clC (cluster C) double crochet 3 stitches together into the next stitch or space (see page 52).

clD (cluster D) 2 dc in next stitch.

PATTERN 4

PATTERN 1

PATTERN 2

PATTERN 3

PATTERN 1

Silver Grey

(make 18)

Using yarn C and 4mm (US G-6, UK 8) hook, make 31 sts using long tail foundation method.

ROW 1 (RS)
1 sc in each st (31 sts).

ROW 2 (WS)
1 sc in each st.

ROW 3
1 dc in each of first 3 sts, (clA, 1 dc in each of next 3 sts) seven times.

ROW 4
1 sc in each st.

ROW 5
1 dc in first st, (clA, 1 dc in each of next 3 sts) seven times, clA, 1 dc in last st.

ROWS 6–24
Rep rows 2–5 a further four times, then rows 2–4 once more.

Fasten off and weave in ends.

BORDER

Join yarn C with a sl st to top right corner of last row in second st, 29 sc, [1 sc, ch 2, 1 sc] in last st of row, turn and work 29 sc evenly along left side, turn, [1 sc, ch 2, 1 sc] in first foundation st, 29 sc along foundation row, [1 sc, ch 2, 1 sc] in last st of foundation row, turn and work 29 sc evenly up right side, turn, [1 sc, ch 2, 1 sc] in first st of top row, join with a sl st (31 sts along each side, 2-ch sp in each corner). PM in each corner 2-ch sp.

Pattern 1 Chart

PATTERN 2

Vintage Green

(make 8)

This pattern starts with a WS row.

Using yarn D and 4mm (US G-6, UK 8) hook, make 31 sts using long tail foundation method.

ROW 1 (WS)
1 sc in each st (31 sts).

ROW 2 (RS)
1 sc in each st.

ROW 3
1 sc in each st.

ROW 4
1 sc in first st, (clB in next st, 1 sc in next st) fifteen times.

ROWS 5–41
Rep rows 1–4 a further nine times, then row 1 once more.

Fasten off and weave in ends.

Turn your work so that the even numbered rows are at the front. This is considered the RS row for joining.

BORDER

Work as Border for Pattern 1 (see page 63) using yarn D.

Pattern 2 Chart

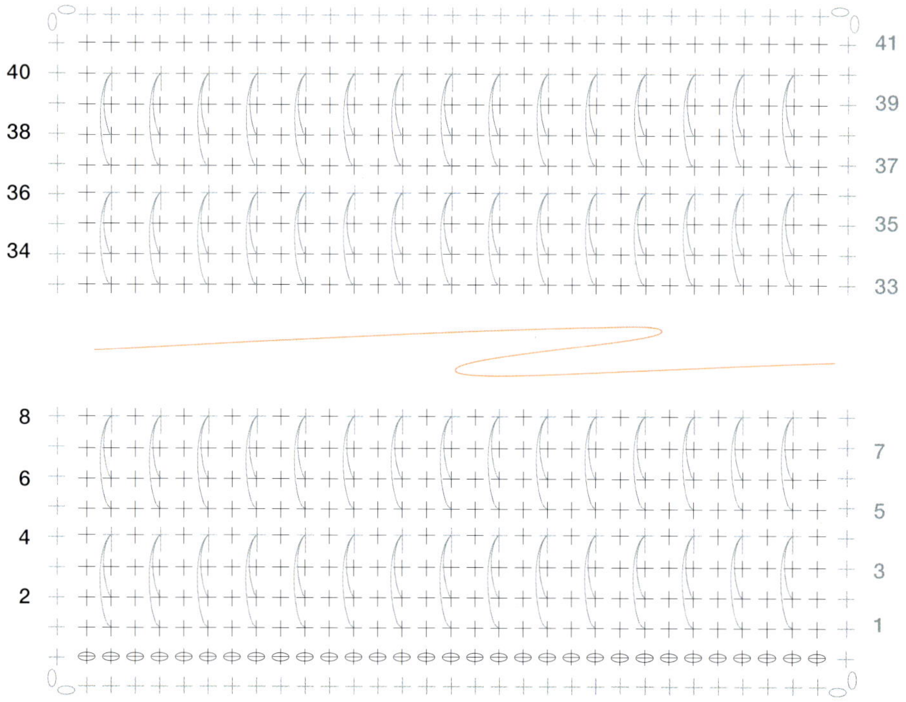

1

2

3

4

5

6

7

→

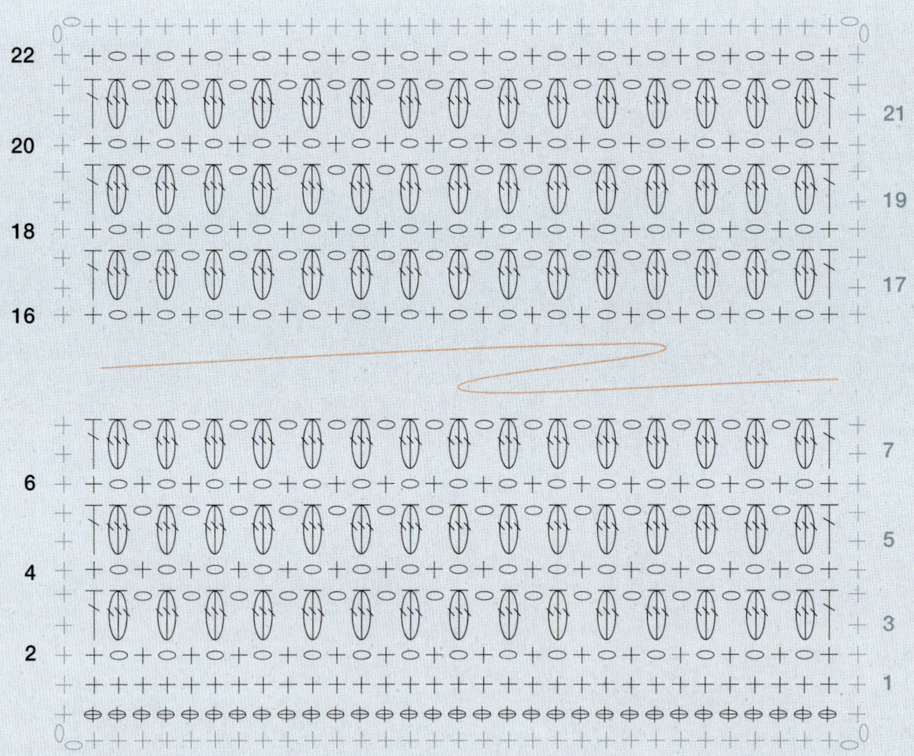

Pattern 3 Chart

Blue Grey

PATTERN 3

(make 5)

Using yarn B and 5mm (US G-8, UK 6) hook, make 31 sts using long tail foundation method.

ROW 1 (RS)
1 sc in each st (31 sts).

ROW 2 (WS)
1 sc in first st, (ch 1, sk 1 sc, 1 sc in next st) fifteen times.

ROW 3
1 dc in first st, (clC in ch sp, ch 1, sk 1 sc) fourteen times, clC in ch sp, 1 dc in last st.

ROW 4
1 sc in first st, (ch 1, sk clC, 1 sc in next ch sp) fourteen times, ch 1, sk clC, 1 sc in last st.

ROWS 5–22
Rep rows 3 and 4 a further nine times.

Fasten off and weave in ends.

BORDER

Work as Border for Pattern 1 (see page 63) using yarn B.

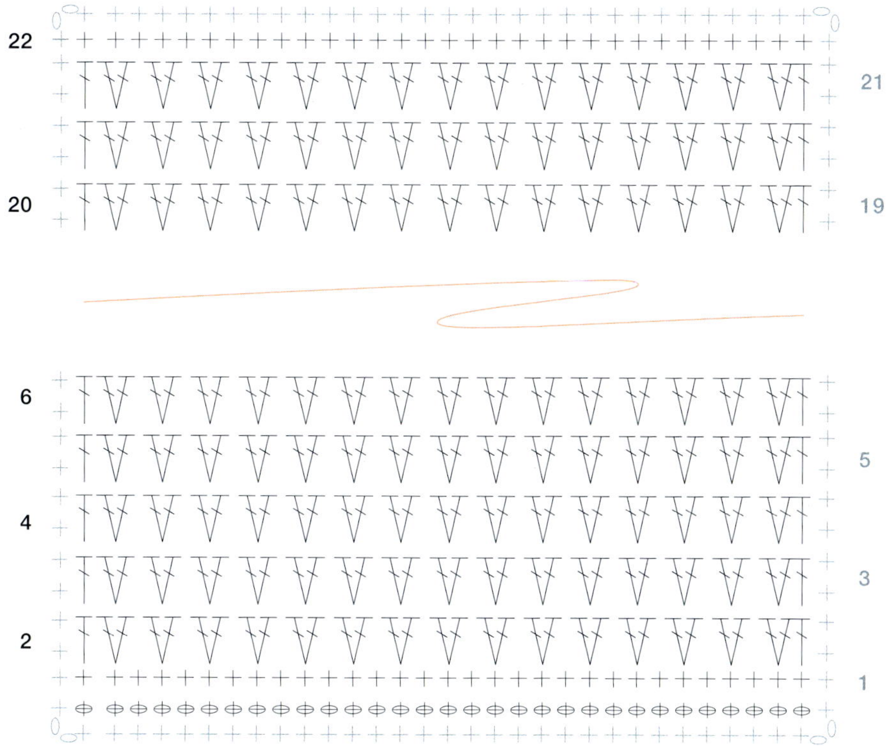

Pattern 4 Chart

Vintage Pink

PATTERN 4

(make 4)

Using yarn A and 4mm (US G-6, UK 8) hook, make 31 sts using long tail foundation method.

ROW 1 (RS)

1 sc in each st (31 sts).

ROW 2 (WS)

1 dc in first st, (clD in next st, sk 1 st) fourteen times, clD, 1 dc in last st.

ROW 3

1 dc in first st, (clD in sp between 2 dc of next clD) fifteen times, 1 dc in last st.

ROWS 4–21

Rep row 3 a further eighteen times.

ROW 22

1 sc in first st, (1 sc in sp between 2 dc of next clD, 1 sc in the sp between next two clD) fourteen times, 1 sc in sp between 2 dc of next clD, 1 sc in last st.

Fasten off and weave in ends.

BORDER

Work as Border for Pattern 1 (see page 63) using yarn A.

Silver Grey

JOINING

Lay out the squares according to the Joining chart below, making sure the RS of each square is facing upwards. Join the squares together in vertical strips first, then join the strips together horizontally. Place the first two squares (one from each of first two strips) wrong sides together.

Using yarn C and 4mm (US G-6, UK 8) hook, join both squares at one corner with an sc, sc blo through next st of both squares, sc blo through each pair of sts to corner space, sc in both corner spaces, join the corner spaces of the next two squares in the same way and the pairs of sts in the same way.

Where they are already joined, work 1 sc in first corner space, (1 ch, 1 sc) in next corner space. Do not work in the sts already made when joining the long strips.

Continue in this way until you have joined two sets of seven blocks together.

Fasten off and weave in ends.

Join strips 3 and 4 together in the same way, then join strip 5 to strip 4 and finally join strips 1 and 2 to 3, 4 and 5.

Fasten off and weave in ends.

Joining Chart

1	4	1	2	1
4	1	2	1	3
1	2	1	3	1
2	1	3	1	2
1	3	1	2	1
3	1	2	1	4
1	2	1	4	1

OUTER BORDER

ROUND 1 (RS)
With RS facing, using 4mm (UK 8, US 6) hook, join yarn C in any st, work in sc evenly along edges, work [1 sc, ch 2, 1 sc] in corner spaces, work 1 sc in corner space, 1 sc in seam, 1 sc in next corner space at the joins between squares, join with a sl st at end.

Fasten off.

ROUND 2 (WS)
Turn, join yarn B in any st, work in sc along edges, work [1 sc, ch 2, 1 sc] in corner spaces, join with a sl st at end.

ROUND 3 (RS)
Turn, work in sc along edges, work [1 sc, ch 2, 1 sc] in corner spaces.

ROUND 4 (WS)
Turn, work in sc along edges, work [1 sc, ch 2, 1 sc] in corner spaces.

Fasten off.

ROUND 5 (RS)
Turn, join yarn B in st above the first seam after a corner, sl st in same st, *clB in next st. 1 sc in next st, rep from * to the end of the side.

NOTE
The last clB will only be worked as far as picking up one loop in row below, not the second loop, 1 sc in last st of this side, [1 sc, ch 2, 1 sc] in corner space, 1 sc in next st, 1 shortened clB in next st,1 sc in next st, *clB in next st. 1 sc in next st, rep from * to the end of the side.

Continue in the same way around, working each corner in the same manner, join with a sl st.

ROUND 6 (WS)
Turn, work in sc along edges, work [1 sc, ch 2, 1 sc] in corner spaces.

Fasten off.

ROUND 7 (RS)
Turn, join yarn C in any st, work in sc along edges, work 3 sc in corner spaces, join with a sl st at end.

Fasten off and weave in ends.

Outer Border Chart A

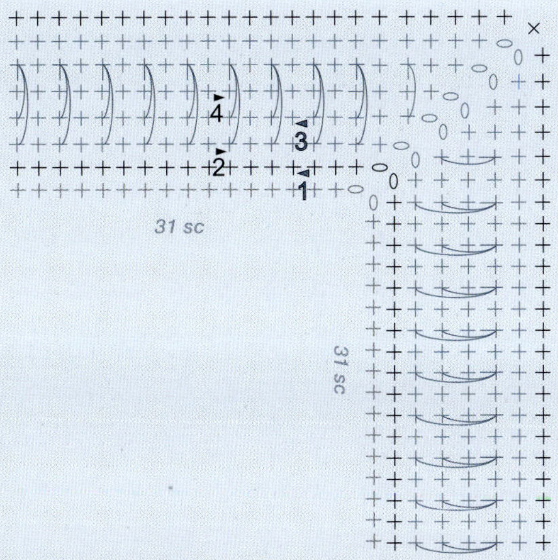

Outer Border Chart B

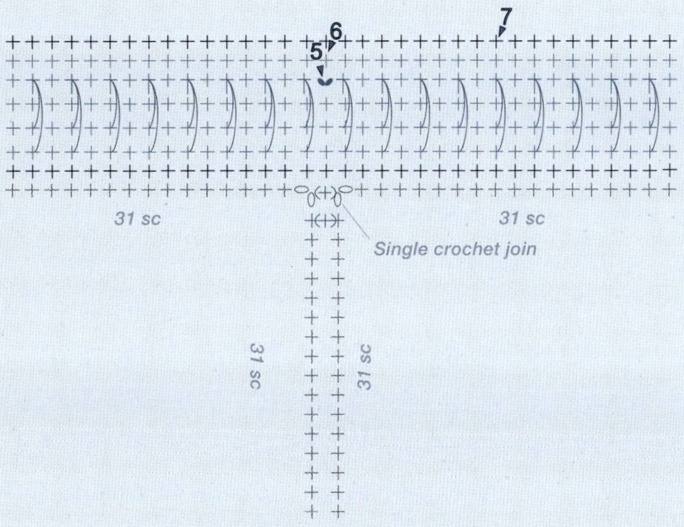

Light and Airy

This open throw features a calming wave motif within the strips, and is edged with a decorative pointed border.

The wide strips, featuring the main motif, are joined using a delicate filet stitch.

MATERIALS

19 balls of **Durable Cotton No. 6**
1–3-ply (lace weight) cotton yarn
(100g/3½oz/300m/328yd) in White (009)

TOOLS

2.5mm (US B-1/C-2, UK 12) crochet hook
Tapestry needle

FINISHED SIZE

Approx. 180 × 220cm (71 × 87in)

- 1 middle strip is 33cm (13in) wide; the points are 12.5cm (5in) high
- 1 repetition measures 19cm (7½in) high

DIFFICULTY LEVEL

Medium

KEY

- *long tail foundation*
- *slip stitch*
- *chain*
- *single crochet*
- *double crochet*
- *linked treble crochet*
- *linked double treble crochet*

PATTERN NOTES

The blanket is made up of strips worked in rows, which means you will need to turn the work at the end of each row. This is not in the written instructions.

There are a number of middle strips flanked by side strips. The two side strips mirror each other, hence there are 3 different strip pattern sections.

The first st in each row is created by working × ch, depending on the st that it replaces (e.g. dc = 3 ch). This is not in the written instructions.

The blue (odd) row numbers indicate rounds that are crocheted on the RS of the work. When joining, ensure that all of the RS are facing the front.

STITCHES AND ABBREVIATIONS USED

ch	chain(s)
ch sp(s)	chain space(s)
dc	double crochet
RS	right side
sc	single crochet
sk	skip (miss)
sl st	slip stitch
st(s)	stitch(es)
WS	wrong side
yo	yarn over hook

SPECIAL STITCHES

Ltr Linked treble crochet

Wrap the yarn over the hook twice, insert the hook through two diagonal bars of the last dc in the row, pull up a loop, ch 1, (yo, pull through two loops) three times.

Start each subsequent linked stitch in the diagonal bars of the previous linked stitch.

Ldtr Linked double treble crochet

Wrap the yarn over the hook three times, insert the hook through two diagonal bars of the last dc in the row, pull up a loop, ch 1, (yo, pull through two loops) four times.

Start each subsequent linked stitch in the ch 1 of the previous foundation stitch.

MIDDLE STRIP

(make 3)

Make 7 sts using long tail foundation method.

INCREASE SECTION

ROW 1 (RS)
1 dc in each st (7 sts).

ROW 2 (WS)
1 dc in each st, ch 6.

ROW 3
1 dc in each of 6 ch, 1 dc in next dc, ch 3, sk 2 sts, 1 sc in next st, ch 3, sk 2 sts, 1 dc in next st, 6 Ltr (19 sts).

ROW 4
1 dc in each of next 7 sts, ch 5, sk [ch 3, 1 sc, ch 3], 1 dc in each of next 7 sts, ch 6.

ROW 5
1 dc in each of 6 ch, 1 dc in next dc, *ch 3, sk 2 sts, 1 sc in next st, ch 3, sk 2 sts, 1 dc in next st, rep from * to end, 6 Ltr (31 sts).

ROW 6
1 dc in each of next 7 sts, *ch 5, sk [ch 3, 1 sc, ch 3], 1 dc in next st, rep from * to last 6 sts, 1 dc in each of last 6 sts, ch 6.

ROWS 7–13
Rep rows 5 and 6 three more times, then row 5 once (79 sts).

ROW 14
1 dc in each of next 7 sts, *ch 5, sk [ch 3, 1 sc, ch 3], 1 dc in next st, rep from * to last 6 sts, 1 dc in each of last 6 sts, ch 2.

MAIN SECTION

ROW 15
1 dc in first ch, ch 1, sk ch 1, 1 dc in next st, (ch 3, sk 2 sts, 1 sc in next st, ch 3, sk 2 sts, 1 dc in next st) six times, 1 dc in each of next 12 sts, (ch 3, sk 2 sts, 1 sc in next st, ch 3, sk 2 sts, 1 dc in next st) five times, ch 1, 1 Ltr (83 sts).

ROW 16
1 dc in first st, ch 1, sk ch 1, 1 dc in next st, (ch 5, sk [ch 3, 1 sc, ch 3], 1 dc in next st) five times, 1 dc in each of next 12 sts, (ch 5, sk [ch 3, 1 sc, ch 3], 1 dc in next st) six times, ch 1, sk ch 1, 1 dc in last st.

Linked treble crochet

Wrap the yarn over the hook twice.

Insert the hook through 2 loops at the bottom of the last dc from the row below.

Pull up a loop.

Yarn over, pull through 2 loops, yarn over, pull through 2 loops.

Yarn over, pull through 2 loops.

Start each subsequent linked stitch in the bottom loop of the previous linked stitch from the row below.

ROW 17
1 dc in first st, ch 1, sk ch 1, 1 dc in next st, (ch 3, sk 2 sts, 1 sc in next st, ch 3, sk 2 sts, 1 dc in next st) four times, 1 dc in each of next 12 sts, (ch 3, sk 2 sts, 1 sc in next st, ch 3, sk 2 sts, 1 dc in next st) seven times, ch 1, sk ch 1, 1 dc in last st.

ROW 18
1 dc in first st, ch 1, sk ch 1, 1 dc in next st, (ch 5, sk [ch 3, 1 sc, ch 3], 1 dc in next st) seven times, 1 dc in each of next 12 sts, (ch 5, sk [ch 3, 1 sc, ch 3], 1 dc in next st) four times, ch 1, sk ch 1, 1 dc in last st.

ROW 19
1 dc in first st, ch 1, sk ch 1, 1 dc in next st, (ch 3, sk 2 sts, 1 sc in next st, ch 3, sk 2 sts, 1 dc in next st) three times, 1 dc in each of next 12 sts, (ch 3, sk 2 sts, 1 sc in next st, ch 3, sk 2 sts, 1 dc in next st) eight times, ch 1, sk ch 1, 1 dc in last st.

ROW 20
1 dc in first st, ch 1, sk ch 1, 1 dc in next st, (ch 5, sk [ch 3, 1 sc, ch 3], 1 dc in next st) eight times, 1 dc in each of next 12 sts, (ch 5, sk [ch 3, 1 sc, ch 3], 1 dc in next st) three times, ch 1, sk ch 1, 1 dc in last st.

ROW 21
1 dc in first st, ch 1, sk ch 1, 1 dc in next st, (ch 3, sk 2 sts, 1 sc in next st, ch 3, sk 2 sts, 1 dc in next st) three times, 1 dc in each of next 12 sts, (ch 3, sk 2 sts, 1 sc in next st, ch 3, sk 2 sts, 1 dc in next st) twice, 1 dc in each of next 18 sts, (ch 3, sk 2 sts, 1 sc in next st, ch 3, sk 2 sts, 1 dc in next st) three times, ch 1, sk ch 1, 1 dc in last st.

ROW 22
1 dc in first dc, ch 1, sk ch 1, 1 dc in next st, (ch 5, sk [ch 3, 1 sc, ch 3], 1 dc in next st) three times, 1 dc in each of next 18 sts, (ch 5, sk [ch 3, 1 sc, ch 3], 1 dc in next st) twice.

1 dc in each of next 12 sts, (ch 5, sk [ch 3, 1 sc, ch 3], 1 dc in next st) three times, ch 1, sk ch 1, 1 dc in last st.

ROW 23
1 dc in first st, ch 1, sk ch 1, 1 dc in next st, (ch 3, sk 2 sts, 1 sc in next st, ch 3, sk 2 sts, 1 dc in next st) three times, 1 dc in each of next 12 sts, ch 3, sk 2 sts, 1 sc in next st, ch 3, sk 2 sts, 1 dc in next st, 1 dc in each of next 6 sts, (ch 3, sk 2 sts, 1 sc in next st, ch 3, sk 2 sts, 1 dc in next st) twice, 1 dc in each of next 12 sts, (ch 3, sk 2 sts, 1 sc in next st, ch 3, sk 2 sts, 1 dc in next st) twice, ch 1, sk ch 1, 1 dc in last st.

ROW 24
1 dc in first st, ch 1, sk ch 1, 1 dc in next st, (ch 5, sk [ch 3, 1 sc, ch 3], 1 dc in next st) twice, 1 dc in each of next 12 sts, (ch 5, sk [ch 3, 1 sc, ch 3], 1 dc in next st) twice, 1 dc in each of next 6 sts, ch 5, sk (ch 3, 1 sc, ch 3), 1 dc in next st, 1 dc in each of next 12 sts, (ch 5, sk [ch 3, 1 sc, ch 3], 1 dc in next st) three times, ch 1, sk ch 1, 1 dc in last st.

ROWS 25 AND 26
Rep rows 23 and 24 once.

ROW 27
1 dc in first st, ch 1, sk ch 1, 1 dc in next st, (ch 3, sk 2 sts, 1 sc in next st, ch 3, sk 2 sts, 1 dc in next st) three times, 1 dc in each of next 12 sts, (ch 3, sk 2 sts, 1 sc in next st, ch 3, sk 2 sts, 1 dc in next st) twice, 1 dc in each of next 6 sts, ch 3, sk 2 sts, 1 sc in next st, ch 3, sk 2 sts, 1 dc in next st, 1 dc in each of next 12 sts, (ch 3, sk 2 sts, 1 sc in next st, ch 3, sk 2 sts, 1 dc in next st) twice, ch 1, sk ch 1, 1 dc in last st.

ROW 28
1 dc in first st, ch 1, sk ch 1, 1 dc in next st, (ch 5, sk [ch 3, 1 sc, ch 3], 1 dc in next st) twice, 1 dc in each of next 12 sts, ch 5, sk (ch 3, 1 sc, ch 3), 1 dc in next st, 1 dc in each of next 6 sts, (ch 5, sk [ch 3, 1 sc, ch 3], 1 dc in next st) twice, 1 dc in each of next 12 sts, (ch 5, sk [ch 3, 1 sc, ch 3], 1 dc in next st) three times, ch 1, sk ch 1, 1 dc in last st.

ROW 29
1 dc in first st, ch 1, sk ch 1, 1 dc in next st, (ch 3, sk 2 sts, 1 sc in next st, ch 3, sk 2 sts, 1 dc in next st) four times, 1 dc in each of next 18 sts, (ch 3, sk 2 sts, 1 sc in next st, ch 3, sk 2 sts, 1 dc in next st) twice, 1 dc in each of next 12 sts, (ch 3, sk 2 sts, 1 sc in next st, ch 3, sk 2 sts, 1 dc in next st) twice, ch 1, sk ch 1, 1 dc in last st.

ROW 30
1 dc in first st, ch 1, sk ch 1, 1 dc in next st, (ch 5, sk [ch 3, 1 sc, ch 3], 1 dc in next st) twice, 1 dc in each of next 12 sts, (ch 5, sk [ch 3, 1 sc, ch 3], 1 dc in next st) twice, 1 dc in each of next 18 sts, (ch 5, sk [ch 3, 1 sc, ch 3], 1 dc in next st) four times, ch 1, sk ch 1, 1 dc in last st.

⟶

ROW 31
1 dc in first st, ch 1, sk ch 1, 1 dc in next st, (ch 3, sk 2 sts, 1 sc in next st, ch 3, sk 2 sts, 1 dc in next st) nine times, 1 dc in each of next 12 sts, (ch 3, sk 2 sts, 1 sc in next st, ch 3, sk 2 sts, 1 dc in next st) twice, ch 1, sk ch 1, 1 dc in last st.

ROW 32
1 dc in first st, ch 1, sk ch 1, 1 dc in next st, (ch 5, sk [ch 3, 1 sc, ch 3], 1 dc in next st) twice, 1 dc in each of next 12 sts, (ch 5, sk [ch 3, 1 sc, ch 3], 1 dc in next st) nine times, ch 1, sk ch 1, 1 dc in last st.

ROW 33
1 dc in first st, ch 1, sk ch 1, 1 dc in next st, (ch 3, sk 2 sts, 1 sc in next st, ch 3, sk 2 sts, 1 dc in next st) eight times, 1 dc in each of next 12 sts, (ch 3, sk 2 sts, 1 sc in next st, ch 3, sk 2 sts, 1 dc in next st) three times, ch 1, sk ch 1, 1 dc in last st.

ROW 34
1 dc in first st, ch 1, sk ch 1, 1 dc in next st, (ch 5, sk [ch 3, 1 sc, ch 3], 1 dc in next st) three times, 1 dc in each of next 12 sts, (ch 5, sk [ch 3, 1 sc, ch 3], 1 dc in next st) eight times, ch 1, sk ch 1, 1 dc in last st.

ROW 35
1 dc in first st, ch 1, sk ch 1, 1 dc in next st, (ch 3, sk 2 sts, 1 sc in next st, ch 3, sk 2 sts, 1 dc in next st) six times, 1 dc in each of next 12 sts, (ch 3, sk 2 sts, 1 sc in next st, ch 3, sk 2 sts, 1 dc in next st) five times, ch 1, sk ch 1, 1 dc in last st.

ROW 36
1 dc in first st, ch 1, sk ch 1, 1 dc in next st, (ch 5, sk [ch 3, 1 sc, ch 3], 1 dc in next st) five times, 1 dc in each of next 12 sts, (ch 5, sk [ch 3, 1 sc, ch 3], 1 dc in next st) six times, ch 1, sk ch 1, 1 dc in last st.

ROWS 37–236
Rep rows 17–36 ten more times.

DECREASE SECTION

ROW A (RS)
Sk first st, 1 sl st in 1-ch sp, [1 sl st, 1 dc] in next st, 1 dc in each of next 5 ch, 1 dc in next dc, (ch 3, sk 2 sts, 1 sc in next st, ch 3, sk 2 sts, 1 dc in next st) eleven times, 1 dc in each of next 5 ch, 1 dc in next dc (79 sts).

ROW B (WS)
1 dc in each of next 7 sts, (ch 5, sk [ch 3, 1 sc, ch 3], 1 dc in next st) eleven times, 1 dc in each of last 6 sts.

ROW C
Sk first st, 1 sl st in each of next 5 sts, (1 sl st, 1 dc) in next st, 1 dc in each of next 5 ch, 1 dc in next st, *ch 3, sk 2 sts, 1 sc in next st, ch 3, sk 2 sts, 1 dc in next st, rep from * to last 5-ch sp and 7 dc, 1 dc in each of next 5 ch, 1 dc in next dc (67 sts).

ROW D
1 dc in each of next 7 sts, *(ch 5, sk [ch 3, 1 sc, ch 3], 1 dc in next st), rep from * to last 6 sts, 1 dc in each of last 6 sts.

ROWS E–L
Rep rows C and D four more times (19 sts).

ROW M
Sk first st, 1 sl st in each of next 5 sts, (1 sl st, 1 dc) in next st, 1 dc in each of next 5 ch, 1 dc in next st (7 sts).

ROW N
1 dc in each of next 7 sts.

Fasten off and weave in ends.

RIGHT STRIP

Make 7 sts using long tail foundation method.

INCREASE SECTION

ROWS 1 (RS)–13
As for rows 1–13 of Middle Strip (79 sts) at end of row 13.

ROW 14
1 dc in each of next 7 sts, (ch 5, sk [ch 3, 1 sc, ch 3], 1 dc in next st) eleven times, 1 dc in each of last 6 sts, ch 6.

MAIN SECTION

ROW 15 (RS)
1 dc in each of 6 ch, 1 dc in next dc, (ch 3, sk 2 sts, 1 sc in next st, ch 3, sk 2 sts, 1 dc in next st) six times, 1 dc in each of next 12 sts, (ch 3, sk 2 sts, 1 sc in next st, ch 3, sk 2 sts, 1 dc in next st) five times, ch 1, 1 Ltr (87 sts).

ROW 16 (WS)
1 dc in first st, ch 1, sk ch 1, 1 dc in next st, (ch 5, sk [ch 3, 1 sc, ch 3], 1 dc in next st) five times, 1 dc in each of next 12 sts, (ch 5, sk [ch 3, 1 sc, ch 3], 1 dc in next st) six times, 1 dc in each of last 6 sts, ch 6.

ROW 17
1 dc in each of 6 ch, 1 dc in next dc, (ch 3, sk 2 sts, 1 sc in next st, ch 3, sk 2 sts, 1 dc in next st) nine times, 1 dc in each of next 12 sts, (ch 3, sk 2 sts, 1 sc in next st, ch 3, sk 2 sts, 1 dc in next st) three times, ch 1, sk ch 1, 1 dc in last st (93 sts).

ROW 18
1 dc in first st, ch 1, sk ch 1, 1 dc in next st, (ch 5, sk [ch 3, 1 sc, ch 3], 1 dc in next st) three times, 1 dc in each of next 12 sts, (ch 5, sk [ch 3, 1 sc, ch 3], 1 dc in next st) nine times, 1 dc in each of last 6 sts, ch 6.

ROW 19
1 dc in each of 6 ch, 1 dc in next dc, ch 3, sk 2 sts, 1 sc in next st, ch 3, sk 2 sts, 1 dc in next st, 1 dc in each of next 6 sts, (ch 3, sk 2 sts, 1 sc in next st, ch 3, sk 2 sts, 1 dc in next st) nine times, 1 dc in each of next 12 sts, (ch 3, sk 2 sts, 1 sc in next st, ch 3, sk 2 sts, 1 dc in next st) twice, ch 1, sk ch 1, 1 dc in last st (99 sts).

ROW 20
1 dc in first st, ch 1, sk ch 1, 1 dc in next st, (ch 5, sk [ch 3, 1 sc, ch 3], 1 dc in next st) twice, 1 dc in each of next 12 sts, (ch 5, sk [ch 3, 1 sc, ch 3], 1 dc in next st) nine times, 1 dc in each of next 6 sts, ch 5, sk [ch 3, 1 sc, ch 3], 1 dc in next st, 1 dc in each of last 6 sts.

ROW 21
Sk first st, 1 sl st in each of next 5 sts, (1 sl st, 1 dc) in next st, 1 dc in each of next 5 ch, 1 dc in next st, (ch 3, sk 2 sts, 1 sc in next st, ch 3, sk 2 sts, 1 dc in next st) five times, 1 dc in each of next 18 sts, (ch 3, sk 2 sts, 1 sc in next st, ch 3, sk 2 sts, 1 dc in next st) twice, 1 dc in each of next 12 dc, (ch 3, sk 2 sts, 1 sc in next st, ch 3, sk 2 sts, 1 dc in next st) twice, ch 1, sk ch 1, 1 dc in last st (93 sts).

ROW 22
1 dc in first st, ch 1, sk ch 1, 1 dc in next st, (ch 5, sk [ch 3, 1 sc, ch 3], 1 dc in next st) twice, 1 dc in each of next 12 sts, (ch 5, sk [ch 3, 1 sc, ch 3], 1 dc in next st) twice, 1 dc in each of next 18 sts, (ch 5, sk [ch 3, 1 sc, ch 3], 1 dc in next st) five times, 1 dc in each of last 6 sts.

→

ROW 23
Sk first st, 1 sl st in each of next 5 sts, (1 sl st, 1 dc) in next st, 1 dc in each of next 5 ch, 1 dc in next st, (ch 3, sk 2 sts, 1 sc in next st, ch 3, sk 2 sts, 1 dc in next st) three times, 1 dc in each of next 12 sts, (ch 3, sk 2 sts, 1 sc in next st, ch 3, sk 2 sts, 1 dc in next st) twice, 1 dc in each of next 6 sts, ch 3, sk 2 sts, 1 sc in next st, ch 3, sk 2 sts, 1 dc in next st, 1 dc in each of next 12 sts, (ch 3, sk 2 sts, 1 sc in next st, ch 3, sk 2 sts, 1 dc in next st) twice, ch 1, sk ch 1, 1 dc in last st (87 sts).

ROW 24
1 dc in first st, ch 1, sk ch 1, 1 dc in next st, (ch 5, sk [ch 3, 1 sc, ch 3], 1 dc in next st) twice, 1 dc in each of next 12 sts, ch 5, sk [ch 3, 1 sc, ch 3], 1 dc in next st, 1 dc in each of next 6 sts (ch 5, sk [ch 3, 1 sc, ch 3], 1 dc in next st) twice, 1 dc in each of next 12 sts, (ch 5, sk [ch 3, 1 sc, ch 3], 1 dc in next st) three times, 1 dc in each of last 6 sts.

ROW 25
Sk first st, 1 sl st in each of next 5 sts, (1 sl st, 1 dc) in next st, 1 dc in each of next 5 ch, 1 dc in next st, (ch 3, sk 2 sts, 1 sc in next st, ch 3, sk 2 sts, 1 dc in next st) twice, 1 dc in each of next 12 sts, (ch 3, sk 2 sts, 1 sc in next st, ch 3, sk 2 sts, 1 dc in next st) twice, 1 dc in each of next 6 sts, ch 3, sk 2 sts, 1 sc in next st, ch 3, sk 2 sts, 1 dc in next st, 1 dc in each of next 12 sts, (ch 3, sk 2 sts, 1 sc in next st, ch 3, sk 2 sts, 1 dc in next st) twice, ch 1, sk ch 1, 1 dc in last st (81 sts).

ROW 26
1 dc in first st, ch 1, sk ch 1, 1 dc in next st, (ch 5, sk [ch 3, 1 sc, ch 3], 1 dc in next st) twice, 1 dc in each of next 12 sts, ch 5, sk [ch 3, 1 sc, ch 3], 1 dc in next st, 1 dc in each of next 6 sts, (ch 5, sk [ch 3, 1 sc, ch 3], 1 dc in next st) twice, 1 dc in each of next 12 sts, (ch 5, sk [ch 3, 1 sc, ch 3], 1 dc in next st) twice, 1 dc in each of last 6 sts.

ROW 27
Sk first st, 1 sl st in each of next 5 sts, (1 sl st, 1 dc) in next st, 1 dc in each of next 5 ch, 1 dc in next st, ch 3, sk 2 sts, 1 sc in next st, ch 3, sk 2 sts, 1 dc in next st, 1 dc in each of next 12 sts, ch 3, sk 2 sts, 1 sc in next st, ch 3, sk 2 sts, 1 dc in next st, 1 dc in each of next 6 sts, (ch 3, sk 2 sts, 1 sc in next st, ch 3, sk 2 sts, 1 dc in next st) twice, 1 dc in each of next 12 sts, (ch 3, sk 2 sts, 1 sc in next st, ch 3, sk 2 sts, 1 dc in next st) twice, ch 1, sk ch 1, 1 dc in last st (75 sts).

ROW 28
1 dc in first st, ch 1, sk ch 1, 1 dc in next st, (ch 5, sk [ch 3, 1 sc, ch 3], 1 dc in next st) twice, 1 dc in each of next 12 sts, (ch 5, sk [ch 3, 1 sc, ch 3], 1 dc in next st) twice, 1 dc in each of next 6 sts, ch 5, sk [ch 3, 1 sc, ch 3], 1 dc in next st, 1 dc in each of next 12 sts, ch 5, sk [ch 3, 1 sc, ch 3], 1 dc in next st, 1 dc in each of last 6 sts, ch 6.

ROW 29
1 dc in each of 6 ch, 1 dc in next dc, (ch 3, sk 2 sts, 1 sc in next st, ch 3, sk 2 sts, 1 dc in next st) twice, 1 dc in each of next 12 sts, (ch 3, sk 2 sts, 1 sc in next st, ch 3, sk 2 sts, 1 dc in next st) twice, 1 dc in each of next 18 sts, (ch 3, sk 2 sts, 1 sc in next st, ch 3, sk 2 sts, 1 dc in next st) three times, ch 1, sk ch 1, 1 dc in last st (81 sts).

ROW 30
1 dc in first st, ch 1, sk ch 1, 1 dc in next st, (ch 5, sk [ch 3, 1 sc, ch 3], 1 dc in next st) three times, 1 dc in each of next 18 sts, (ch 5, sk [ch 3, 1 sc, ch 3], 1 dc in next st) twice, 1 dc in each of next 12 sts, (ch 5, sk [ch 3, 1 sc, ch 3], 1 dc in next st) twice, 1 dc in each of last 6 sts, ch 6.

ROW 31
1 dc in each of 6 ch, 1 dc in next dc, (ch 3, sk 2 sts, 1 sc in next st, ch 3, sk 2 sts, 1 dc in next st) three times, 1 dc in each of next 12 sts, (ch 3, sk 2 sts, 1 sc in next st, ch 3, sk 2 sts, 1 dc in next st) eight times, ch 1, sk ch 1, 1 dc in last st (87 sts).

ROW 32
1 dc in first st, ch 1, sk ch 1, 1 dc in next st, (ch 5, sk [ch 3, 1 sc, ch 3], 1 dc in next st) eight times, 1 dc in each of next 12 sts, (ch 5, sk [ch 3, 1 sc, ch 3], 1 dc in next st) three times, 1 dc in each of last 6 sts, ch 6.

ROW 33
1 dc in each of 6 ch, 1 dc in next dc, (ch 3, sk 2 sts, 1 sc in next st, ch 3, sk 2 sts, 1 dc in next st) five times, 1 dc in each of next 12 sts, (ch 3, sk 2 sts, 1 sc in next st, ch 3, sk 2 sts, 1 dc in next st) seven times, ch 1, sk ch 1, 1 dc in last st (93 sts).

ROW 34
1 dc in first st, ch 1, sk ch 1, 1 dc in next st, (ch 5, sk [ch 3, 1 sc, ch 3], 1 dc in next st) seven times, 1 dc in each of next 12 sts, (ch 5, sk [ch 3, 1 sc, ch 3], 1 dc in next st) five times, 1 dc in each of last 6 sts, ch 6.

ROW 35
1 dc in each of 6 ch, 1 dc in next dc, ch 3, sk 2 sts, 1 sc in next st, ch 3, sk 2 sts, 1 dc in next st, 1 dc in each of next 6 sts, (ch 3, sk 2 sts, 1 sc in next st, ch 3, sk 2 sts, 1 dc in next st) six times, 1 dc in each of next 12 sts, (ch 3, sk 2 sts, 1 sc in next st, ch 3, sk 2 sts, 1 dc in next st) five times, ch 1, sk ch 1, 1 dc in last st (99 sts).

ROW 36
1 dc in first st, ch 1, sk ch 1, 1 dc in next st, (ch 5, sk [ch 3, 1 sc, ch 3], 1 dc in next st) five times, 1 dc in each of next 12 sts, (ch 5, sk [ch 3, 1 sc, ch 3], 1 dc in next st) six times, 1 dc in each of next 6 sts, ch 5, sk [ch 3, 1 sc, ch 3], 1 dc in next st, 1 dc in each of last 6 sts, ch 6.

ROW 37
1 dc in each of 6 ch, 1 dc in next dc, ch 3, sk 2 sts, 1 sc in next st, ch 3, sk 2 sts, 1 dc in next st, 1 dc in each of next 6 sts, (ch 3, sk 2 sts, 1 sc in next st, ch 3, sk 2 sts, 1 dc in next st) nine times, 1 dc in each of next 12 sts, (ch 3, sk 2 sts, 1 sc in next st, ch 3, sk 2 sts, 1 dc in next st) three times, ch 1, sk ch 1, 1 dc in last st (105 sts).

ROW 38
1 dc in first st, ch 1, sk ch 1, 1 dc in next st, (ch 5, sk [ch 3, 1 sc, ch 3], 1 dc in next st) three times, 1 dc in each of next 12 sts, (ch 5, sk [ch 3, 1 sc, ch 3], 1 dc in next st) nine times, 1 dc in each of next 6 sts, ch 5, sk [ch 3, 1 sc, ch 3], 1 dc in next st, 1 dc in each of last 6 sts.

ROWS 39–233
Rep rows 19–38 nine more times, then rows 19–33 once more, working each row 19 with 'sk first st, 1 sl st in each of next 5 sts, (1 sl st, 1 dc) in next st', at the beginning instead of '1 dc in each of 6 ch, 1 dc in next dc'.

ROW 234
1 dc in first st, ch 1, sk ch 1, 1 dc in next st, (ch 5, sk [ch 3, 1 sc, ch 3], 1 dc in next st) seven times, 1 dc in each of next 12 sts, (ch 5, sk [ch 3, 1 sc, ch 3], 1 dc in next st) five times, 1 dc in each of last 6 sts.

DECREASE SECTION

ROW A
Sk first st, 1 sl st in each of next 5 sts, (1 sl st, 1 dc) in next st, 1 dc in each of next 5 ch, 1 dc in next st, (ch 3, sk 2 sts, 1 sc in next st, ch 3, sk 2 sts, 1 dc in next st) six times, 1 dc in each of next 12 sts, (ch 3, sk 2 sts, 1 sc in next st, ch 3, sk 2 sts, 1 dc in next st) five times, ch 1, sk ch 1, 1 dc in last st (87 sts).

ROW B
1 dc in first st, ch 1, sk ch 1, 1 dc in next st, (ch 5, sk [ch 3, 1 sc, ch 3], 1 dc in next st) five times, 1 dc in each of next 12 sts, (ch 5, sk [ch 3, 1 sc, ch 3], 1 dc in next st) six times, 1 dc in each of last 6 sts.

ROW C
Sk first st, 1 sl st in each of next 5 sts, (1 sl st, 1 dc) in next st, 1 dc in each of next 5 ch, 1 dc in next st, (ch 3, sk 2 sts, 1 sc in next st, ch 3, sk 2 sts, 1 dc in next st) eleven times, 1 dc in each of next 6 sts (79 sts).

⟶

ROW D
1 dc in each of next 7 sts, (ch 5, sk [ch 3, 1 sc, ch 3], 1 dc in next st) eleven times, 1 dc in each of the last 6 sts.

ROW E
Sk first st, 1 sl st in each of next 5 sts, (1 sl st, 1 dc) in next st, 1 dc in each of next 5 ch, 1 dc in next st, *ch 3, sk 2 sts, 1 sc in next st, ch 3, sk 2 sts, 1 dc in next st, rep from * to last 5-ch sp and 7 dc, 1 dc in each of next 5 ch, 1 dc in next dc (67 sts).

ROW F
1 dc in each of next 7 sts, *(ch 5, sk [ch 3, 1 sc, ch 3], 1 dc in next st), rep from * to last 6 sts, 1 dc in each of last 6 sts.

ROWS G–N
Rep rows E and F four more times (19 sts).

ROW O
Sk first st, 1 sl st in each of next 5 sts, (1 sl st, 1 dc) in next st, 1 dc in each of next 5 ch, 1 dc in next st, turn (7 sts).

ROW P
1 dc in each of next 7 sts.

Fasten off and weave in ends.

LEFT STRIP

Make 7 sts using long tail foundation method.

INCREASE SECTION

ROWS 1 (RS)–14 (WS)
As for rows 1–14 of Middle Strip (79 sts at end of row 13).

MAIN SECTION

ROW 15
1 dc in first ch, ch 1, sk ch 1, 1 dc in next st, (ch 3, sk 2 sts, 1 sc in next st, ch 3, sk 2 sts, 1 dc in next st) five times, 1 dc in each of next 12 sts, (ch 3, sk 2 sts, 1 sc in next st, ch 3, sk 2 sts, 1 dc in next st) six times, 6 Ltr (87 sts).

ROW 16
1 dc in each of next 7 sts, (ch 5, sk [ch 3, 1 sc, ch 3], 1 dc in next st) six times, 1 dc in each of next 12 sts, (ch 5, sk [ch 3, 1 sc, ch 3], 1 dc in next st) five times, ch 1, sk ch 1, 1 dc in last st.

ROW 17
1 dc in first st, ch 1, sk ch 1, 1 dc in next st, (ch 3, sk 2 sts, 1 sc in next st, ch 3, sk 2 sts, 1 dc in next st) seven times, 1 dc in each of next 12 sts, (ch 3, sk 2 sts, 1 sc in next st, ch 3, sk 2 sts, 1 dc in next st) five times, 6 Ltr (93 sts).

ROW 18
1 dc in each of next 7 sts, (ch 5, sk [ch 3, 1 sc, ch 3], 1 dc in next st) five times, 1 dc in each of next 12 sts, (ch 5, sk [ch 3, 1 sc, ch 3], 1 dc in next st) seven times, ch 1, sk ch 1, 1 dc in last st.

ROW 19
1 dc in first st, ch 1, sk ch 1, 1 dc in next st, (ch 3, sk 2 sts, 1 sc in next st, ch 3, sk 2 sts, 1 dc in next st) eight times, 1 dc in each of next 12 sts, (ch 3, sk 2 sts, 1 sc in next st, ch 3, sk 2 sts, 1 dc in next st) three times, 1 dc in each of next 6 sts, ch 3, sk 2 sts, 1 sc in next st, ch 3, sk 2 sts, 1 dc in next st, 6 Ltr (99 sts).

ROW 20
1 dc in each of next 7 sts, ch 5, sk [ch 3, 1 sc, ch 3], 1 dc in next st, 1 dc in each of next 6 sts, (ch 5, sk [ch 3, 1 sc, ch 3], 1 dc in next st) three times, 1 dc in each of next 12 sts, (ch 5, sk [ch 3, 1 sc, ch 3], 1 dc in next st) eight times, ch 1, sk ch 1, 1 dc in last st.

ROW 21
1 dc in first st, ch 1, sk ch 1, 1 dc in next st, (ch 3, sk 2 sts, 1 sc in next st, ch 3, sk 2 sts, 1 dc in next st) three times, 1 dc in each of next 18 sts, (ch 3, sk 2 sts, 1 sc in next st, ch 3, sk 2 sts, 1 dc in next st) twice, 1 dc in each of next 12 sts, (ch 3, sk 2 sts, 1 sc in next st, ch 3, sk 2 sts, 1 dc in next st) four times, 1 dc in each of next 5 ch, 1 dc in next dc (93 sts).

ROW 22
1 dc in each of next 7 sts, (ch 5, sk [ch 3, 1 sc, ch 3], 1 dc in next st) four times, 1 dc in each of next 12 sts, (ch 5, sk [ch 3, 1 sc, ch 3], 1 dc in next st) twice, 1 dc in each of next 18 sts, (ch 5, sk [ch 3, 1 sc, ch 3], 1 dc in next st) three times, ch 1, sk ch 1, 1 dc in last st.

ROW 23
1 dc in first st, ch 1, sk ch 1, 1 dc in next st, (ch 3, sk 2 sts, 1 sc in next st, ch 3, sk 2 sts, 1 dc in next st) twice, 1 dc in each of next 12 sts, (ch 3, sk 2 sts, 1 sc in next st, ch 3, sk 2 sts, 1 dc in next st) twice, 1 dc in each of next 6 sts, ch 3, sk 2 sts, 1 sc in next st, ch 3, sk 2 sts, 1 dc in next st, 1 dc in each of next 12 sts, (ch 3, sk 2 sts, 1 sc in next st, ch 3, sk 2 sts, 1 dc in next st) three times, 1 dc in each of next 5 ch, 1 dc in next dc (87 sts).

ROW 24
1 dc in each of next 7 sts, (ch 5, sk [ch 3, 1 sc, ch 3], 1 dc in next st) three times, 1 dc in each of next 12 sts, ch 5, sk [ch 3, 1 sc, ch 3], 1 dc in next st, 1 dc in each of next 6 sts, (ch 5, sk [ch 3, 1 sc, ch 3], 1 dc in next st) twice, 1 dc in each of next 12 sts, (ch 5, sk [ch 3, 1 sc, ch 3], 1 dc in next st) twice, ch 1, sk ch 1, 1 dc in last st.

ROW 25
1 dc in first st, ch 1, sk ch 1, 1 dc in next st, (ch 3, sk 2 sts, 1 sc in next st, ch 3, sk 2 sts, 1 dc in next st) twice, 1 dc in each of next 12 sts, (ch 3, sk 2 sts, 1 sc in next st, ch 3, sk 2 sts, 1 dc in next st) twice, 1 dc in each of next 6 sts, ch 3, sk 2 sts, 1 sc in next st, ch 3, sk 2 sts, 1 dc in next st, 1 dc in each of next 12 sts, (ch 3, sk 2 sts, 1 sc in next st, ch 3, sk 2 sts, 1 dc in next st) twice, 1 dc in each of next 5 ch, 1 dc in next dc (81 sts).

ROW 26
1 dc in each of next 7 sts, (ch 5, sk [ch 3, 1 sc, ch 3], 1 dc in next st) twice, 1 dc in each of next 12 sts, ch 5, sk [ch 3, 1 sc, ch 3], 1 dc in next st, 1 dc in each of next 6 sts, (ch 5, sk [ch 3, 1 sc, ch 3], 1 dc in next st) twice, 1 dc in each of next 12 sts, (ch 5, sk [ch 3, 1 sc, ch 3], 1 dc in next st) twice, ch 1, sk ch 1, 1 dc in last st.

ROW 27
1 dc in first st, ch 1, sk ch 1, 1 dc in next st, (ch 3, sk 2 sts, 1 sc in next st, ch 3, sk 2 sts, 1 dc in next st) twice, 1 dc in each of next 12 sts, ch 3, sk 2 sts, 1 sc in next st, ch 3, sk 2 sts, 1 dc in next st, 1 dc in each of next 6 sts, (ch 3, sk 2 dc, 1 sc in next st, ch 3, sk 2 dc, 1 dc in next st) twice, 1 dc in each of next 12 sts, ch 3, sk 2 sts, 1 sc in next st, ch 3, sk 2 sts, 1 dc in next st, 1 dc in each of next 5 ch, 1 dc in next dc (75 sts).

ROW 28
1 dc in each of next 7 sts, ch 5, sk [ch 3, 1 sc, ch 3], 1 dc in next st, 1 dc in each of next 12 sts, (ch 5, sk [ch 3, 1 sc, ch 3], 1 dc in next st) twice, 1 dc in each of next 6 sts, ch 5, sk [ch 3, 1 sc, ch 3], 1 dc in next st, 1 dc in each of next 12 sts, (ch 5, sk [ch 3, 1 sc, ch 3], 1 dc in next st) twice, ch 1, sk ch 1, 1 dc in last st.

ROW 29
1 dc in first st, ch 1, sk ch 1, 1 dc in next st, (ch 3, sk 2 sts, 1 sc in next st, ch 3, sk 2 sts, 1 dc in next st) twice, 1 dc in each of next 12 sts, (ch 3, sk 2 sts, 1 sc in next st, ch 3, sk 2 sts, 1 dc in next st) twice, 1 dc in each of next 18 sts, (ch 3, sk 2 sts, 1 sc in next st, ch 3, sk 2 sts, 1 dc in next st) three times, 6 Ltr (81 sts).

ROW 30
1 dc in each of next 7 sts, (ch 5, sk [ch 3, 1 sc, ch 3], 1 dc in next st) three times, 1 dc in each of next 18 sts, (ch 5, sk [ch 3, 1 sc, ch 3], 1 dc in next st) twice, 1 dc in each of next 12 sts, (ch 5, sk [ch 3, 1 sc, ch 3], 1 dc in next st) twice, ch 1, sk ch 1, 1 dc in last st.

⟶

ROW 31
1 dc in first st, ch 1, sk ch 1, 1 dc in next st, (ch 3, sk 2 sts, 1 sc in next st, ch 3, sk 2 sts, 1 dc in next st) twice, 1 dc in each of next 12 sts, (ch 3, sk 2 sts, 1 sc in next st, ch 3, sk 2 sts, 1 dc in next st) nine times, 6 Ltr (87 sts).

ROW 32
1 dc in each of next 7 sts, (ch 5, sk [ch 3, 1 sc, ch 3], 1 dc in next st) nine times, 1 dc in each of next 12 sts, (ch 5, sk [ch 3, 1 sc, ch 3], 1 dc in next st) twice, ch 1, sk ch 1, 1 dc in last st.

ROW 33
1 dc in first st, ch 1, sk ch 1, 1 dc in next st, (ch 3, sk 2 sts, 1 sc in next st, ch 3, sk 2 sts, 1 dc in next st) three times, 1 dc in each of next 12 sts, (ch 3, sk 2 sts, 1 sc in next st, ch 3, sk 2 sts, 1 dc in next st) nine times, 6 Ltr (93 sts).

ROW 34
1 dc in each of next 7 sts, (ch 5, sk [ch 3, 1 sc, ch 3], 1 dc in next st) nine times, 1 dc in each of next 12 sts, (ch 5, sk [ch 3, 1 sc, ch 3], 1 dc in next st) three times, ch 1, sk ch 1, 1 dc in last st.

ROW 35
1 dc in first st, ch 1, sk ch 1, 1 dc in next st, (ch 3, sk 2 sts, 1 sc in next st, ch 3, sk 2 sts, 1 dc in next st) five times, 1 dc in each of next 12 sts, (ch 3, sk 2 sts, 1 sc in next st, ch 3, sk 2 sts, 1 dc in next st) six times, 1 dc in each of next 6 sts, ch 3, sk 2 sts, 1 sc in next st, ch 3, sk 2 sts, 1 dc in next st, 6 Ltr (99 sts).

ROW 36
1 dc in each of next 7 sts, ch 5, sk [ch 3, 1 sc, ch 3], 1 dc in next st, 1 dc in each of next 6 sts, (ch 5, sk [ch 3, 1 sc, ch 3], 1 dc in next st) six times, 1 dc in each of next 12 sts, (ch 5, sk [ch 3, 1 sc, ch 3], 1 dc in next st) five times, ch 1, sk ch 1, 1 dc in last st.

ROW 37
1 dc in first st, ch 1, sk ch 1, 1 dc in next st, (ch 3, sk 2 sts, 1 sc in next st, ch 3, sk 2 sts, 1 dc in next st) seven times, 1 dc in each of next 12 sts, (ch 3, sk 2 sts, 1 sc in next st, ch 3, sk 2 sts, 1 dc in next st) five times, 1 dc in each of next 6 sts, ch 3, sk 2 sts, 1 sc in next st, ch 3, sk 2 sts, 1 dc in next st, 6 Ltr (105 sts).

ROW 38
1 dc in each of next 7 sts, ch 5, sk [ch 3, 1 sc, ch 3], 1 dc in next st, 1 dc in each of next 6 sts, (ch 5, sk [ch 3, 1 sc, ch 3], 1 dc in next st) five times, 1 dc in each of next 12 sts, (ch 5, sk [ch 3, 1 sc, ch 3], 1 dc in next st) seven times, ch 1, sk ch 1, 1 dc in last st.

ROWS 39–234
Rep rows 19–38 nine more times, then rows 19–34 once more, working each row 19 with '1 dc in each of next 5 ch, 1 dc in next dc, turn', at the end instead of '6 Ltr' (93 sts at end of row 234).

DECREASE SECTION

ROW A
1 dc in first st, ch 1, sk ch 1, 1 dc in next st, (ch 3, sk 2 sts, 1 sc in next st, ch 3, sk 2 sts, 1 dc in next st) five times, 1 dc in each of next 12 sts, (ch 3, sk 2 sts, 1 sc in next st, ch 3, sk 2 sts, 1 dc in next st) six times, 1 dc in each of next 5 ch, 1 dc in next dc (87 sts).

ROW B
1 dc in each of next 7 sts, (ch 5, sk [ch 3, 1 sc, ch 3], 1 dc in next st) six times, 1 dc in each of next 12 sts, (ch 5, sk [ch 3, 1 sc, ch 3], 1 dc in next st) five times, ch 1, sk ch 1, 1 dc in last st.

ROW C
Sk first st, 1 sl st in 1-ch sp, (1 sl st, 1 dc) in next st, 1 dc in each of next 5 ch, 1 dc in next dc, (ch 3, sk 2 sts, 1 sc in next st, ch 3, sk 2 sts, 1 dc in next st) eleven times, 1 dc in each of next 5 ch, 1 dc in next dc (79 sts).

ROW D
1 dc in each of next 7 sts, (ch 5, sk [ch 3, 1 sc, ch 3], 1 dc in next st) eleven times, 1 dc in each of last 6 sts.

ROW E
Sk first st, 1 sl st in each of next 5 sts, (1 sl st, 1 dc) in next st, 1 dc in each of next 5 ch, 1 dc in next st, *ch 3, sk 2 sts, 1 sc in next st, ch 3, sk 2 sts, 1 dc in next st, rep from * to last 5-ch sp and 7 dc, 1 dc in each of next 5 ch, 1 dc in next dc (67 sts).

ROW F
1 dc in each of next 7 sts, *(ch 5, sk) [ch 3, 1 sc, ch 3], 1 dc in next st), rep from * to last 6 sts, 1 dc in each of last 6 sts.

ROWS G–N
Rep rows C and D four more times (19 sts).

ROW O
Sk first st, 1 sl st in each of next 5 sts, [1 sl st, 1 dc] in next st, 1 dc in each of next 5 ch, 1 dc in next st, turn (7 sts).

ROW P
1 dc in each of next 7 sts.

Fasten off and weave in ends.

Left Strip Chart

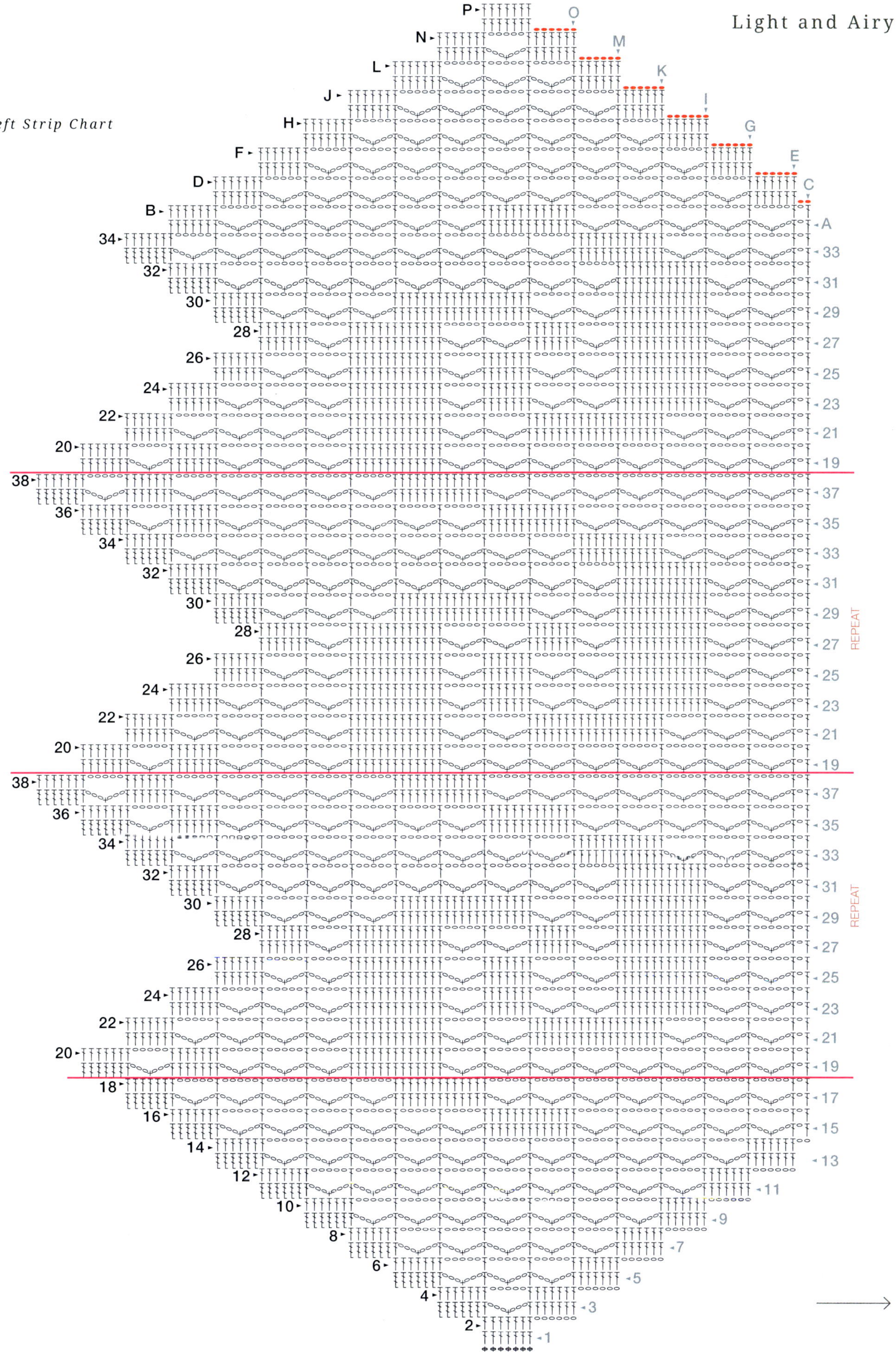

Middle Strip Chart

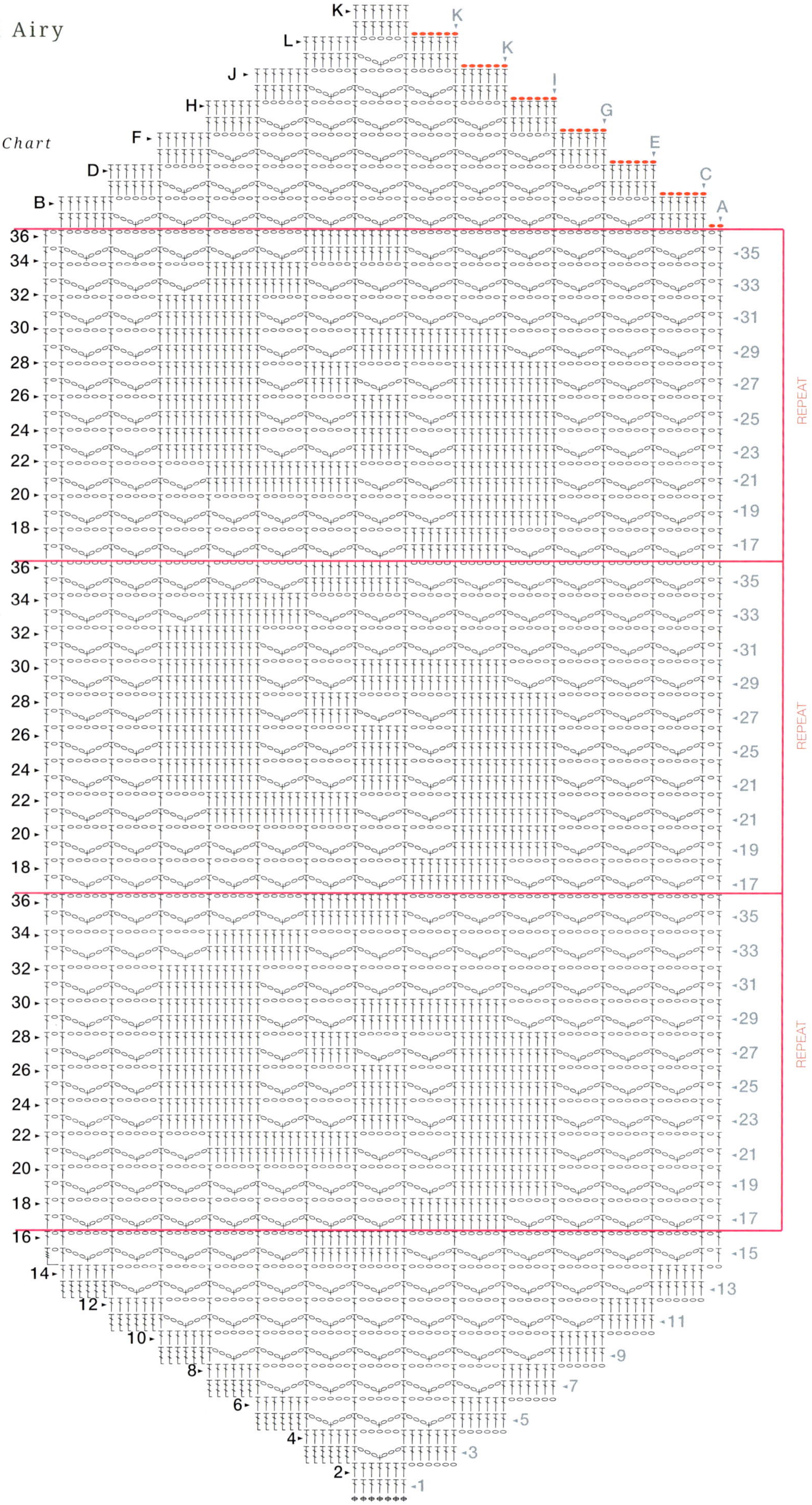

Right Strip Chart

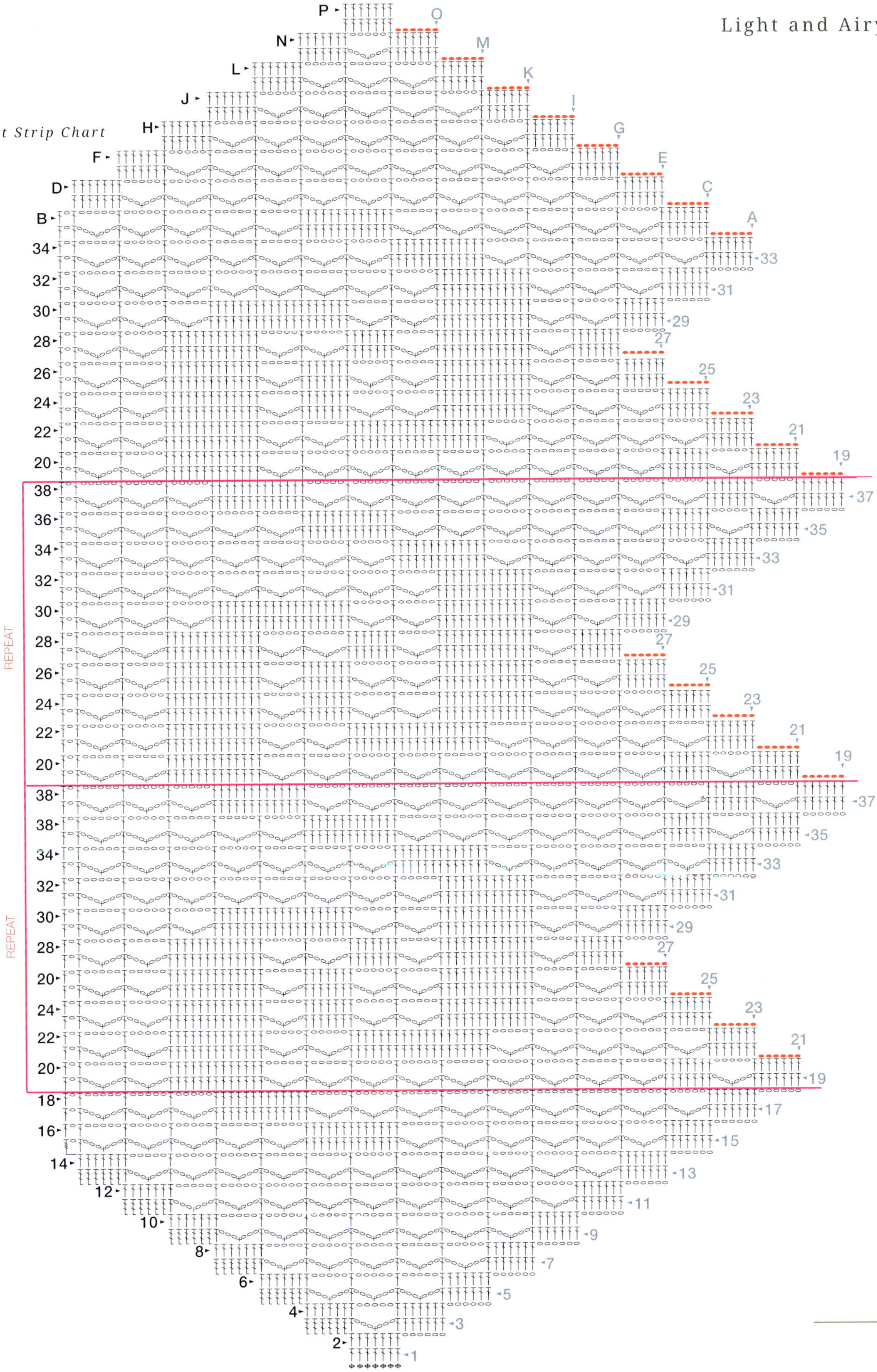

SIDE BORDERS (EACH MIDDLE STRIP)

Right-Hand Side

With RS facing, starting on the right-hand side edge, join yarn in the ch at end of row 14, 1 sc in same st, *1 sc around post of next dc, 1 sc in top of same dc, rep from * to row 36 of the last set of repeated rows.

Left-Hand Side

With RS facing, starting on the left-hand side edge, join yarn in the top of the dc at the start of row 36 in the last set of repeated rows, 1 sc in same place, 1 sc around post of next dc, *1 sc in top of next dc, 1 sc around post of same dc, rep from * to row 15, 1 sc in bottom of Ldtr.

RIGHT-HAND SIDE BORDER (RIGHT STRIP)

With RS facing, starting on the right-hand side edge, join yarn in the ch at end of row 14, 1 sc in same st, *1 sc around post of next dc, 1 sc in top of same dc, rep from * to row B.

LEFT-HAND SIDE BORDER (LEFT STRIP)

With RS facing, starting on the left-hand side edge, join yarn in the top of the dc at the start of row B, 1 sc in same place, 1 sc around post of next dc, *1 sc in top of next dc, 1 sc around post of same dc, rep from * to row 15, 1 sc in bottom of Ltr.

JOINING THE STRIPS

With RS facing, place two strips to be joined next to each other. Join yarn in first sc of left strip, work 1 dc in same st until there are 2 loops left on hook, work 1 dc in first sc of right strip until you have 3 loops left on hook, yo, pull through all 3 loops to join the strips, *ch 1, sk 1 sc of both strips, work 1 dc in next st of left strip until there are 2 loops left on hook, work 1 dc in next st of right strip until you have 3 loops left on hook, yo, pull through all 3 loops to join the strips, rep from * to the end of the strips.

Fasten off and weave in the ends.

Join all the strips in the same way.

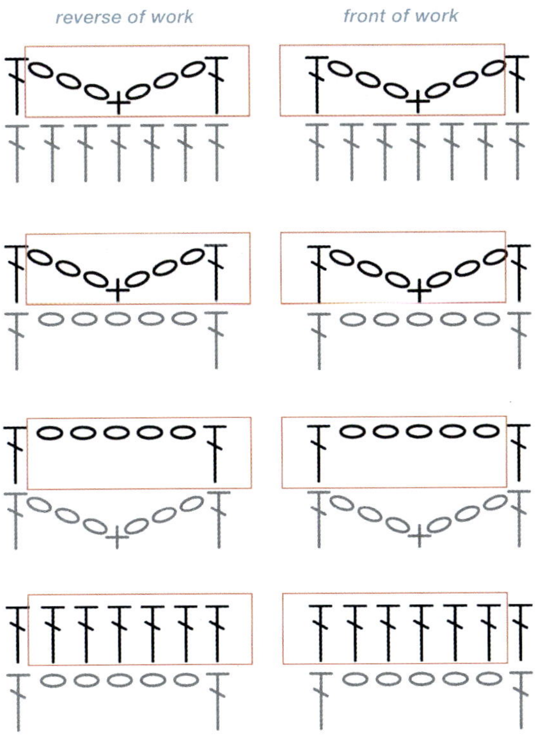

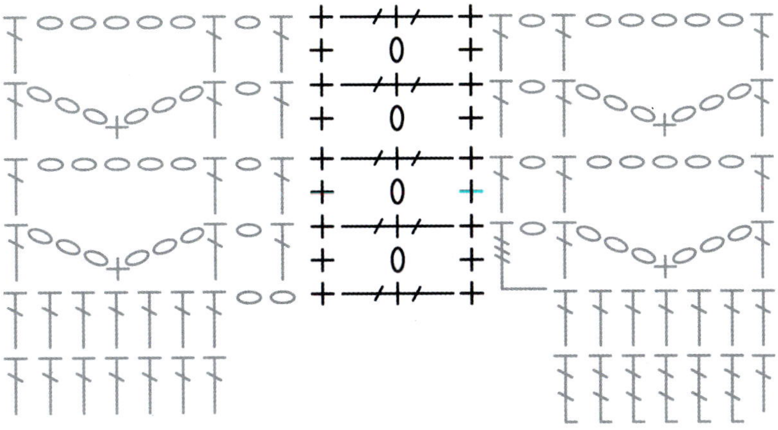

Joining Chart

Magical Motifs

The magic of this blanket is that the triangles it is created from always come together to form hexagons. These hexagons, in turn, create broad strips.

The hexagons form one pattern, while the strips create another.

MATERIALS

20 balls of **Durable Comfy 5-ply (sport) microfibre acrylic yarn** (100g/3½oz/266m/291yd) in Bright Mint (2136)

TOOLS

3.5mm (US 4, UK 9/10) crochet hook

Tapestry needle

FINISHED SIZE

1 triangle

Approx. 25 × 25 × 25cm (10 × 10 × 10in)

Blanket

Approx. 130 × 170cm (51 × 67in)

DIFFICULTY LEVEL

● ○ ○ Easy

KEY

◎ – *magic ring*

⚬ – *chain*

+ – *single crochet*

Ŧ – *double crochet*

PATTERN NOTES

The blanket is worked in the round from the front with no turning.

The first st in each round is created by working × ch, depending on the st that it replaces (e.g. dc = 3 ch). This is not in the written instructions.

STITCHES AND ABBREVIATIONS USED

ch	chain(s)
ch sp(s)	chain space(s)
dc	double crochet
dc3tog	double crochet the next 3 stitches together
sk	skip
sp(s)	space(s)
sl st	slip stitch
st(s)	stitch(es)

ADDITIONAL STITCHES

MATTRESS STITCH

Arrange the pieces according to your chosen colour scheme, RS facing you. Insert the needle from bottom to top, through the back loop of the first stitch of the first (lower) triangle.

Then insert the needle from bottom to top and through the back loop of the first stitch of the second (upper) triangle.

Next, insert the needle from top to bottom-left and then through the back loop of stitch 1 to stitch 2 of the first (lower) triangle. Then, insert the needle from bottom to top-left and through the back loop of stitch 1 to stitch 2 of the second (upper) triangle.

Continue like this until you have formed 10 stitches in total; then carefully pull the yarn so that the seams close and the triangles lie tight against each other. Continue like this to the left corner chain stitch of both triangles. Fasten off.

TRIANGLE

(make 72)

Make a magic ring.

ROUND 1

(7 dc, ch 5) twice in the ring, 7 dc in the ring, ch 2, join round with 1 dc in first st (7 dc per side, 3 corner sps)

ROUND 2

3 dc around joining st, *(1 dc in next st, ch 1, sk 1 st) three times, 1 dc in next st, [3 dc**, ch 5, 3 dc] in ch sp, rep from * once more, then from * to ** once, ch 2, join round with 1 dc in first st (13 sts per side, 3 corner sps).

ROUND 3

3 dc around joining st, *1 dc in each of next 6 sts, ch 1, sk 1 st, 1 dc in each of next 6 sts, [3 dc**, ch 5, 3 dc] in ch sp, rep from * once more, then from * to ** once, ch 2, join round with 1 dc in first st (19 sts per side, 3 corner sps).

ROUND 4

3 dc around joining st, *1 dc in each of next 7 sts, (ch 1, sk 1 st, 1 dc in next st) three times, 1 dc in each of next 6 sts, [3 dc**, ch 5, 3 dc] in ch sp, rep from * once more, then from * to ** once, ch 2, join round with 1 dc in first st (25 sts per side, 3 corner sps).

ROUND 5

3 dc around joining st, *(ch 1, sk 1 st, 1 dc in next st) six times, 1 dc in each of next 2 sts, (ch 1, sk 1 st, 1 dc in next st) five times, ch 1, sk 1 st, [3 dc**, ch 5, 3 dc] in ch sp, rep from * once more, then from * to ** once, ch 2, join round with 1 dc in first st (31 sts per side, 3 corner sps).

ROUND 6

3 dc around joining st, *1 dc in each of next 5 sts, (ch 1, sk 1 st, 1 dc in next st) four times, sk 1 st, 2 dc in next st, 1 dc in next st, 2 dc in next st, sk 1 st, 1 dc in next st, (ch 1, sk 1 st, 1 dc in next st) four times, 1 dc in each of next 4 sts, [3 dc**, ch 5, 3 dc] in ch sp, rep from * once more, then from * to ** once, ch 2, join round with 1 dc in first st (37 sts per side, 3 corner sps).

ROUND 7

3 dc around joining st, *1 dc in each of next 10 sts, (ch 1, sk 1 st, 1 dc in next st) twice, ch 1, sk 2 sts, 2 dc in next st, 1 dc in each of next 3 sts, 2 dc in next st, ch 1, sk 2 sts, 1 dc in next st, (ch 1, sk 1 st, 1 dc in next st) twice, 1 dc in each of next 9 sts, [3 dc**, ch 5, 3 dc] in ch sp, rep from * once more, then from * to ** once, ch 2, join round with 1 dc in first st (43 sts per side, 3 corner sps).

ROUND 8

3 dc around joining st, *1 dc in each of next 15 sts, ch 1, sk 1 st, 1 dc in next st, sk 1 st, 2 dc in next st, 1 dc in each of next 5 sts, 2 dc in next st, sk 1 st, 1 dc in next st, ch 1, sk 1 st, 1 dc in each of next 15 sts, (3 dc, ch 5**, 3 dc) in ch sp, rep from * once more, then from * to ** once, ch 2, sl st in first st (49 sts per side, 3 corner sps).

JOINING

Fasten off and weave in ends.

Join the triangles together using mattress stitch, according to the diagram on page 95, starting with join line 1, then continuing to join in number sequence.

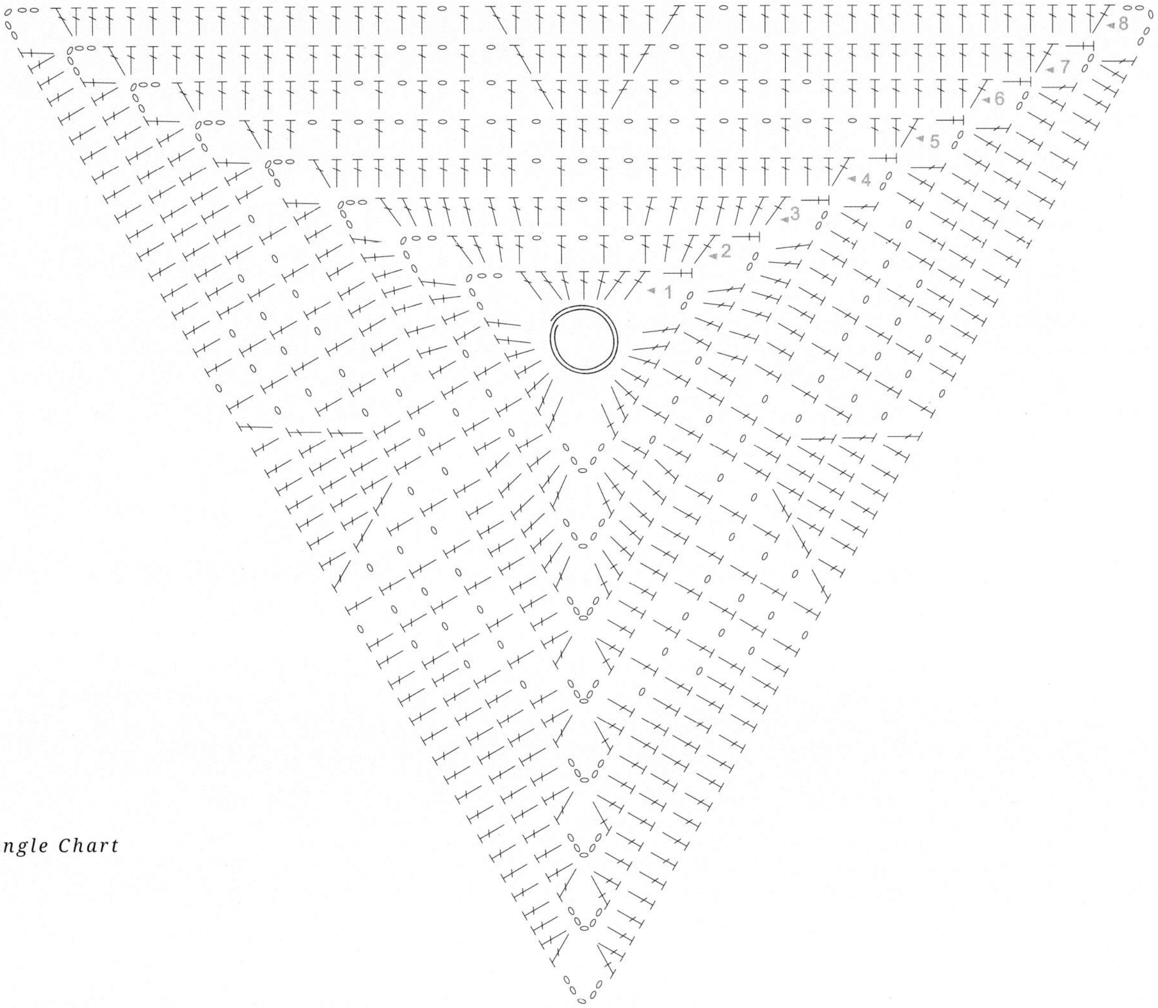

Triangle Chart

BORDER

Crochet the border in the round on RS of the work, joining the yarn in any st. Choose option 1 or option 2 for the top and bottom edges of round 1.

ROUND 1 (ALONG LEFT AND RIGHT SIDES)

1 dc in each st, in outer corners work [3 dc in first ch sp, ch 3, sk the seam, 3 dc in next ch sp], in inside corners work (2 dc in first ch sp, dc3tog worked over first ch sp, middle seam, last ch sp, 2 dc in last ch sp).

ROUND 1 (ALONG TOP AND BOTTOM SIDES)

Option 1

1 dc in each st, where three triangles meet work [2 dc in first ch sp, 1 dc in seam, 1 dc in second ch sp, 1 dc in next seam, 2 dc in last ch sp].

Option 2

1 dc in each st, where three triangles meet work 3 dc in first ch sp, 1 dc in next ch sp, 3 dc in last ch sp.

ROUND 2

1 dc in each st, in outside corners work 5 dc in ch sp, in the inside corners work dc3tog over the sts either side of the previous dc3tog and the dc3tog itself.

Fasten off and weave in ends.

Border Charts

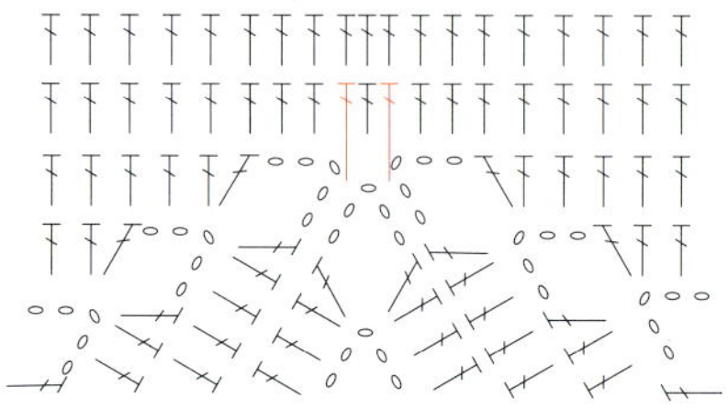

Top and bottom edges
Option 1

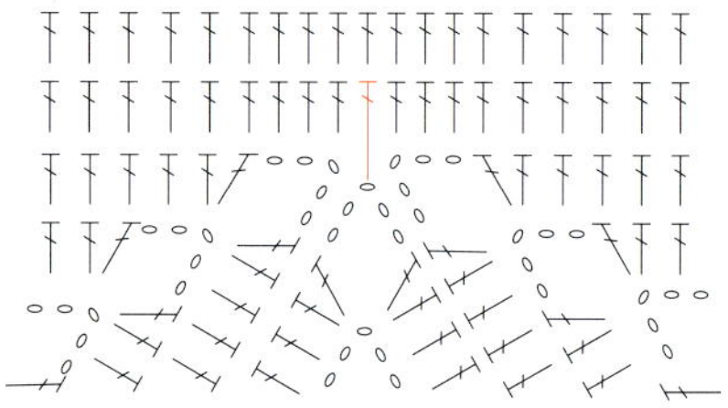

Top and bottom edges
Option 2

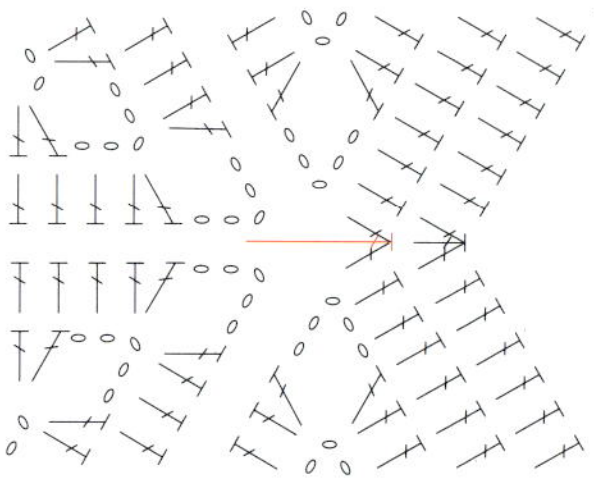

Inside corner

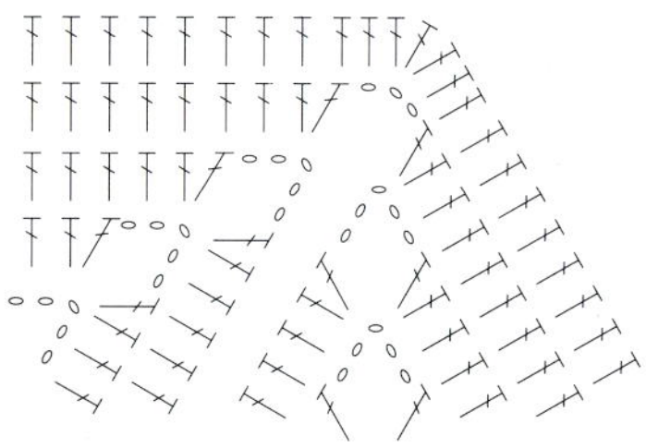

Outside corner

Joining Diagram

Nostalgic Diamonds

Traditional filet crochet is still going strong in the crochet world. We see it here in the form of diamonds, a motif frequently found in old pattern books. When you work the diamonds in different yarns, you can achieve a very different look.

MATERIALS

10 balls of **Durable Knitty 5-ply (sport) microfibre acrylic yarn** (100g/3½oz/266m/291yd) in Light Grey (2232)

TOOLS

3.5mm (US E-4, UK 9/10) crochet hook

Tapestry needle

FINISHED SIZE

Approx. 105 × 160cm (41 × 63in)

DIFFICULTY LEVEL

Easy

KEY

– *chain*

– *double crochet*

PATTERN NOTES

The blanket is worked in rows, and you will need to turn the work at the end of each row.

Use either 2 or 3 ch to turn after every row, depending on your tension. These chs are not listed separately and count as the first stitch.

STITCHES AND ABBREVIATIONS USED

ch	chain(s)
ch sp(s)	chain space(s)
dc	double crochet
RS	right side
sk	skip (miss)
st(s)	stitch(es)
WS	wrong side

BLANKET

Make 167 sts using long tail foundation method.

ROW 1 (RS)

1 dc in each of next 5 sts, *ch 1, sk 1 st, 1 dc in each of next 3 sts, (ch 1, sk 1 st, 1 dc in next st) five times, 1 dc in each of next 2 sts, ch 1, sk 1 st**, 1 dc in each of next 11 sts, rep from * four more times, then from * to ** once, 1 dc in each of last 5 sts (167 sts).

ROW 2 (WS)

1 dc in each of next 4 sts, ch 1, sk 1 st, 1 dc in each of next 5 sts, (ch 1, sk 1 st, 1 dc in next st) four times, 1 dc in each of next 4 sts, ch 1, sk 1 st, *1 dc in each of next 9 sts, ch 1, sk 1 st, 1 dc in each of next 5 sts, (ch 1, sk 1 st, 1 dc in next st) four times, 1 dc in each of next 4 sts, ch 1, sk 1 st, rep from * four more times, 1 dc in each of last 4 sts.

ROW 3

1 dc in each of next 3 sts, *ch 1, sk 1 st, 1 dc in each of next 7 sts, (ch 1, sk 1 st, 1 dc in next st) three times, 1 dc in each of next 6 sts, ch 1, sk 1 st**, 1 dc in each of next 7 sts, rep from * four more times, then from * to ** once, 1 dc in each of last 3 sts.

ROW 4

1 dc in each of next 2 sts, ch 1, sk 1 st, 1 dc in each of next 9 sts, (ch 1, sk 1 st, 1 dc in next st) twice, 1 dc in each of next 8 st, ch 1, sk 1 st, *1 dc in each of next 5 sts, ch 1, sk 1 st, 1 dc in each of next 9 sts, (ch 1, sk 1 st, 1 dc in next st) twice, 1 dc in each of next 8 sts, ch 1, sk 1 st, rep from * four more times, 1 dc in each of last 2 sts.

ROW 5

1 dc in first st, *ch 1, sk 1 st, 1 dc in each of next 11 sts, ch 1, sk 1 st, 1 dc in each of next 11 sts, ch 1, sk 1 st**, 1 dc in each of next 3 sts, rep from * four more times, then from * * to ** once, 1 dc in last st.

ROW 6

As row 4.

ROW 7

As row 3.

ROW 8

As row 2.

ROWS 9–168

Rep rows 1–8 a further 20 times.

Fasten off and weave in ends.

BORDER

NOTE

Crochet in the round on RS of the work. Make sure there is an odd number of stitches on each side after round 1, increase by 1 stitch if necessary.

ROUND 1

Join yarn in to first st in top right corner, 1 dc in each st to last st on top edge, [1 dc, ch 3, 1 dc] in last st, turn to work left side, (1 dc around post of dc, 1 dc in top of next dc) to end of left side, work [1 dc, ch 3, 1 dc] in bottom of last dc, turn to work foundation edge, 1 dc in each st to last st on this edge, [1 dc, ch 3, 1 dc] in last st, turn to work right side, (1 dc around post of dc, 1 dc in top of same dc) to end of right side, end with 1 dc around post of last dc, work [1 dc, ch 3, 1 dc] in top of last dc, join with sl st in next st.

ROUND 2

*(1 dc in first st, ch 1, sk 1 st, 1 dc in next st) rep to last st of this side, [ch 1, 1 dc, ch 3**, 1 dc, ch 1] in corner space, rep from * twice more, then from * to ** once, join with sl st in next st.

ROUND 3

1 dc in each st, 5 dc in each corner space, join with sl st in next st.

Fasten off and weave in the ends.

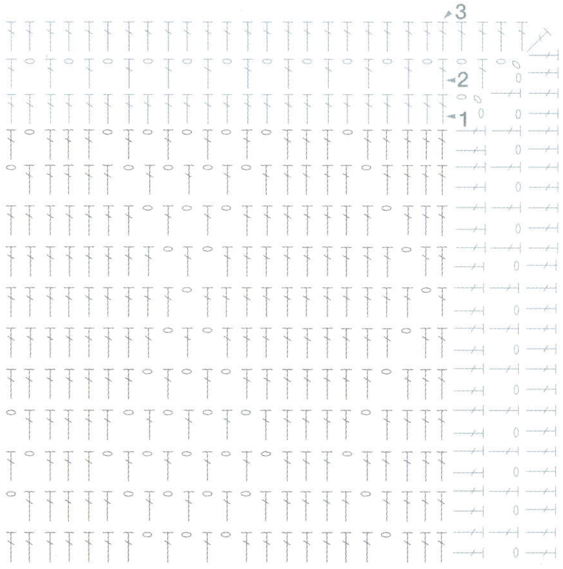

Pattern Repeat Chart

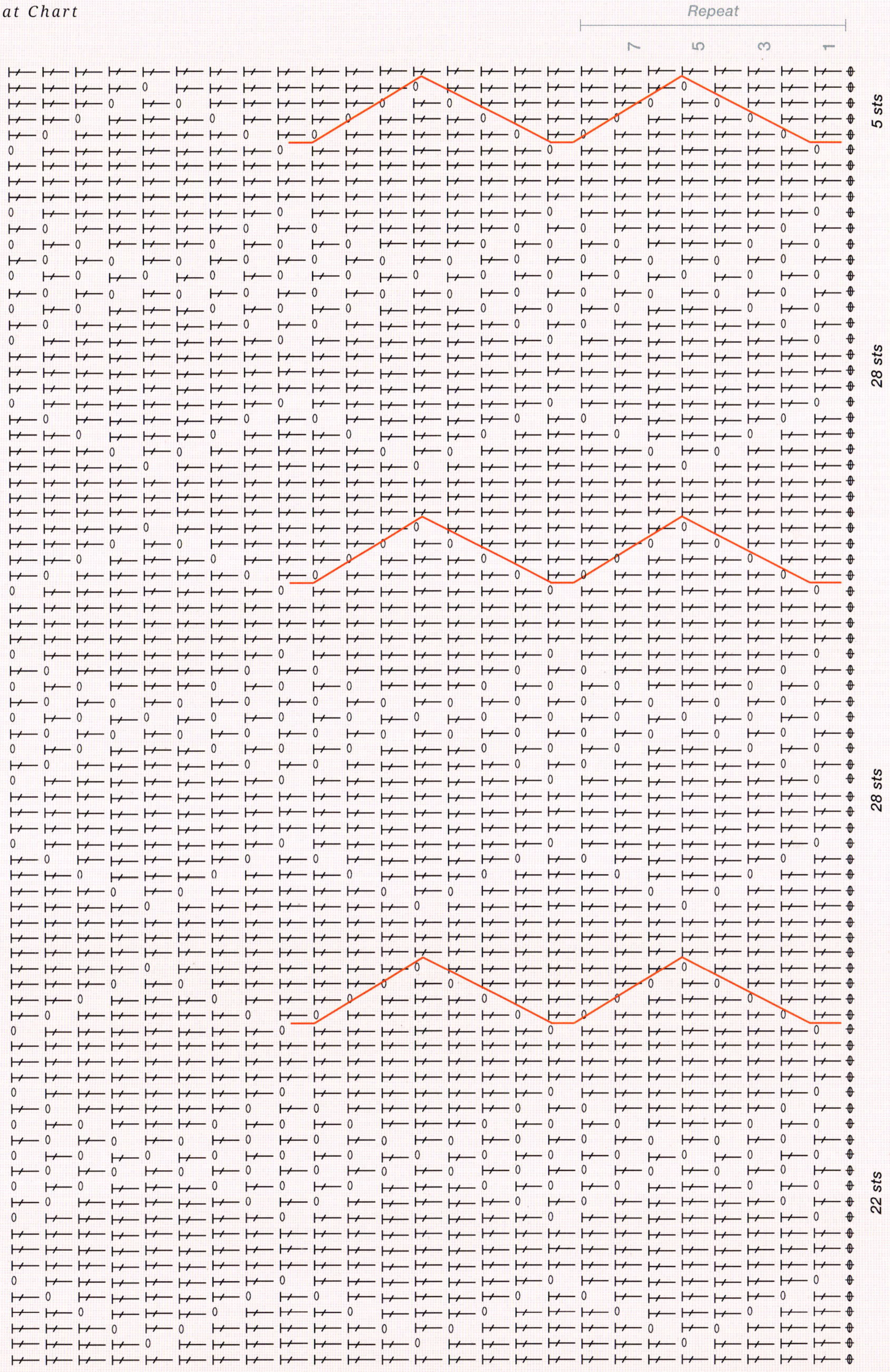

Ocean Waves

This beautiful undulating pattern in blue yarn resembles the waves of the ocean.

A narrower version of this design would make a lovely, wavy scarf to keep you wonderfully warm, perhaps during a walk on the beach!

MATERIALS

16 balls of **Durable Soqs 4-ply (fingering) superwash wool** (50g/1¾oz/210m/230yd) in Turquoise (371)

TOOLS

3mm (US C-2/D-3, UK 11) crochet hook

Tapestry needle

FINISHED SIZE

Approx. 115 × 160cm (45 × 63in)

DIFFICULTY LEVEL

Easy

KEY

- *– long tail foundation*
- *– chain*
- *– single crochet*
- *– double crochet*
- *– double crochet 2 stitches together (dc2tog)*

PATTERN NOTES

The blanket is worked in rows, which means you will need to turn the work at the end of each row. Turns are not included in the written instructions.

Use either 2 or 3 ch to turn after every row, depending on your tension. These chs are not listed separately and count as the first stitch.

To work the dc2tog in this blanket, the hook is placed in two different stitches, which are then joined.

STITCHES AND ABBREVIATIONS USED

ch	chain(s)
ch sp(s)	chain space(s)
dc	double crochet
dc2tog	double crochet the next 2 stitches together
RS	right side
sc	single crochet
sk	skip
st(s)	stitch(es)
WS	wrong side

ADDITIONAL STITCHES

DOUBLE CROCHET 2 TOGETHER (DC2TOG)

*Yarn over, insert hook into next stitch, yarn over and pull through, yarn over and pull through two loops on hook, rep from * once more (three loops on hook), yarn over and pull through all loops on hook.

BLANKET

Work 288 stitches using the long tail foundation.

ROW 1 (RS)

1 dc in each st (288 sts).

ROW 2 (WS)

1 dc in each of first 2 sts, *ch 3, sk 3 sts, (2 dc in next st) twice, ch 3, sk 3 sts**, dc2tog, 1 dc in next st, 2 dc in next st, ch 3, sk 3 sts, 1 sc in next st, ch 3, sk 3 sts, 2 dc in next st, 1 dc in next st, dc2tog, rep from * eleven more times, then from * to ** once,1 dc in each of last 2 sts.

ROW 3

1 dc in each of first 2 sts, ch 3, sk ch 3, 2 dc in next st, 1 dc in each of next 2 sts, 2 dc in next st, ch 3, sk ch 3, *dc2tog, 1 dc in next st, 2 dc in next st, ch 3, 1 sc in sc, ch 3, 2 dc in next st, 1 dc in next st, dc2tog, ch 3, sk ch 3, 2 dc in next st, 1 dc in each of next 2 sts, 2 dc in next st, ch 3, sk ch 3, rep from * eleven more times, 1 dc in each of last 2 sts (340 sts).

ROW 4

1 dc in each of first 2 sts, *ch 3, sk ch 3, 2 dc in next st, 1 dc in each of next 4 sts, 2 dc in next st, ch 3, sk ch 3**, dc2tog, 1 dc in next st, 2 dc in next st, sk [ch 3, 1 sc, ch 3], 2 dc in next st, 1 dc in next st, dc2tog, rep from * eleven more times, then from * to ** once, 1 dc in each of last 2 sts.

ROW 5

1 dc in each of first 2 sts, ch 3, sk ch 3, 2 dc in next st, 1 dc in next st, dc2tog, ch 7, dc2tog, 1 dc in next st, 2 dc in next st, ch 3, sk ch 3, *dc2tog, 1 dc in each of next 4 sts, dc2tog, ch 3, sk ch 3, 2 dc in next st, 1 dc in next st, dc2tog, ch 7, dc2tog, 1 dc in next st, 2 dc in next st, ch 3, sk ch 3, rep from * eleven more times, 1 dc in each of last 2 sts.

ROW 6

1 dc in each of first 2 sts, *ch 3, sk ch 3, 2 dc in next st, 1 dc in next st, dc2tog, ch 3, 1 sc in middle ch of 7-ch sp, ch 3, sk ch 3, dc2tog, 1 dc in next st, 2 dc in next st, ch 3, sk ch 3**, dc2tog, 1 dc in each of next 2 sts, dc2tog, rep from * eleven more times, then from * to ** once, 1 dc in each of last 2 sts.

ROW 7

1 dc in each of first 2 sts, ch 3, sk ch 3, 2 dc in next st, 1 dc in next st, dc2tog, ch 3, sk ch 3, 1 sc in sc, ch 3, sk ch 3, dc2tog, 1 dc in next st, 2 dc in next st, ch 3, sk ch 3, *(dc2tog) twice, ch 3, sk ch 3, 2 dc in next st, 1 dc in next st, dc2tog, ch 3, sk ch 3, 1 sc in sc, ch 3, sk ch 3, dc2tog, 1 dc in next st, 2 dc in next st, ch 3, sk ch 3, rep from * eleven more times, 1 dc in each of last 2 sts.

ROW 8

1 dc in each of first 2 sts, *ch 3, sk ch 3, 1 dc in each of next 4 sts, ch 3, sk ch 3, 1 sc in sc, ch 3, sk ch 3, 1 dc in each of next 4 sts, ch 3, sk ch 3, 1 dc in each of next 2 sts, rep from * twelve more times.

ROW 9

1 dc in each of first 2 sts, ch 3, sk ch 3, dc2tog, 1 dc in next st, 2 dc in next st, ch 3, sk ch 3, 1 sc in next sc, ch 3, sk ch 3, 2 dc in next st, 1 dc in next st, dc2tog, ch 3, sk ch 3, *(2 dc in next st) twice, ch 3, sk ch 3, dc2tog, 1 dc in next st, 2 dc in next st, ch 3, sk ch 3, 1 sc in next sc, ch 3, sk ch 3, 2 dc in next st, 1 dc in next st, dc2tog, ch 3, sk ch 3, rep from * eleven more times, 1 dc in each of last 2 sts.

ROW 10

1 dc in each of first 2 sts, *ch 3, sk ch 3, dc2tog, 1 dc in next st, 2 dc in next st, ch 3, sk ch 3, 1 sc in sc, ch 3, sk ch 3, 2 dc in next st, 1 dc in next st, dc2tog, ch 3, sk ch 3**, 2 dc in next st, 1 dc in each of next 2 sts, 2 dc in next st, rep from * eleven more times, then from * to ** once, 1 dc in each of last 2 sts.

ROW 11
1 dc in each of first 2 sts, ch 3, sk ch 3, dc2tog, 1 dc in next st, 2 dc in next st, sk [ch 3, 1 sc, ch 3], 2 dc in next st, 1 dc in next st, dc2tog, ch 3, sk ch 3, *2 dc in next st, 1 dc in each of next 4 dc, 2 dc in next st, ch 3, sk ch 3, dc2tog, 1 dc in next st, 2 dc in next st, sk [ch 3, 1 sc, ch 3], 2 dc in next st, 1 dc in next st, dc2tog, ch 3, sk ch 3, rep from * eleven more times, 1 dc in each of last 2 sts.

ROW 12
1 dc in each of first 2 sts, *ch 3, sk ch 3, dc2tog, 1 dc in each of next 4 sts, dc2tog, ch 3, sk ch 3**, 2 dc in next st, 1 dc in next st, dc2tog, ch 7, dc2tog, 1 dc in next st, 2 dc in next st, rep from * eleven more times, then from * to ** once, 1 dc in each of last 2 sts.

ROW 13
1 dc in each of first 2 sts, ch 3, sk ch 3, dc2tog, 1 dc in each of next 2 sts, dc2tog, ch 3, sk ch 3, *2 dc in next st, 1 dc in next st, dc2tog, ch 3, 1 sc in middle ch of 7-ch sp, ch 3, sk ch 3, dc2tog, 1 dc in next st, 2 dc in next st, ch 3, sk ch 3, dc2tog, 1 dc in each of next 2 sts, dc2tog, ch 3, sk ch 3, rep from * eleven more times, 1 dc in each of last 2 sts.

ROW 14
1 dc in each of first 2 sts, *ch 3, sk ch 3, (dc2tog) twice, ch 3, sk ch 3**, 2 dc in next st, 1 dc in next st, dc2tog, ch 3, sk ch 3, 1 sc in next sc, ch 3, sk ch 3, dc2tog, 1 dc in next st, 2 dc in next st, rep from * eleven more times, then from * to ** once, 1 dc in each of last 2 sts.

ROW 15
1 dc in each of first 2 sts, ch 3, sk ch 3, 1 dc in each of next 2 sts, ch 3, sk ch 3, *1 dc in each of next 4 sts, ch 3, sk ch 3, 1 sc in next sc, ch 3, sk ch 3, 1 dc in each of next 4 sts, ch 3, sk ch 3, 1 dc in each of next 2 sts, ch 3, sk ch 3, rep from * eleven more times, 1 dc in each of last 2 sts.

ROWS 16–225
Rep rows 2–15 thirteen more times, then rows 2–14 once more, on each row 2 replace each 'sk 3 sts' with 'sk ch 3'.

BORDER

ROW 226 (WS)
1 dc in each st.

Fasten off and weave in ends.

→

Pattern Repeat Chart

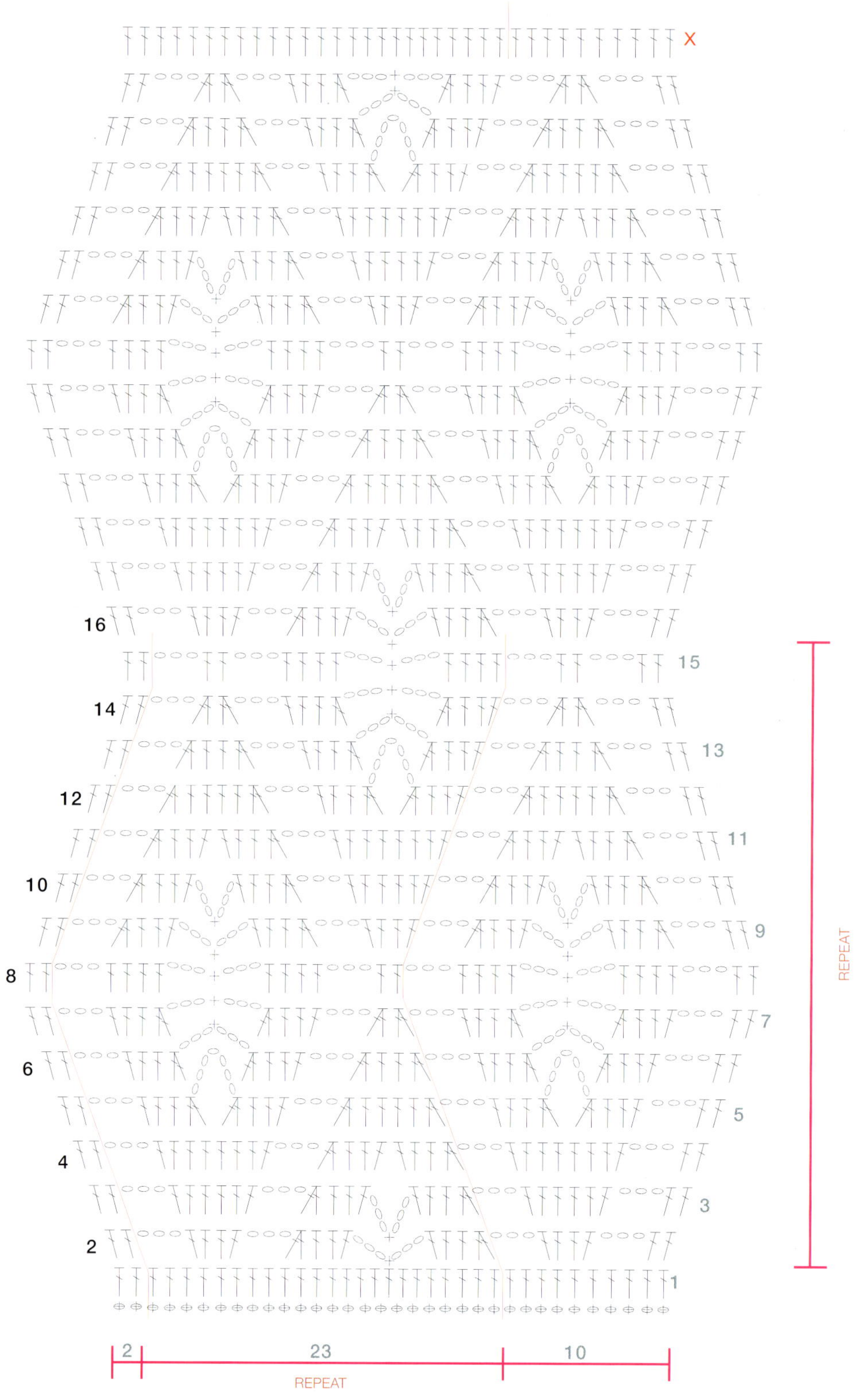

Serene Serenade

To be serene is to be calm yet serious. This blanket embodies those notions, with its light and airy openwork squares that soothe as you crochet. The serious bit comes in the counting, which has to be done accurately!

MATERIALS

19 balls of **Durable Soqs 4-ply (fingering) superwash wool** (50g/1¾oz/210m/230yd) in Lavender Grey (421)

TOOLS

3mm (US C-2/D-3, UK 11) crochet hook

Tapestry needle

FINISHED SIZE

Approx. 135 × 100cm (53 × 39in)

DIFFICULTY LEVEL

Easy

KEY

– long tail foundation

– chain

– single crochet

– half double crochet

– double crochet

– double treble crochet

– cluster (2 double crochets worked in 1 stitch)

– V-stitch (double crochet, 2 ch, double crochet in the same stitch)

PATTERN NOTES

The blanket is worked in rows, which means you will need to turn the work at the end of each row.

Each row starts with 2 ch. These chs are not listed separately and count as the first stitch.

STITCHES AND ABBREVIATIONS USED

ch	chain(s)
ch sp(s)	chain space(s)
cl2	2 double crochets worked in the same st or ch sp
CSq	closed square: cluster in next st, 1 dc in next st or dc
dc	double crochet
OSq	open square: ch 1, sk 1 st, 1 dc in next st or ch sp
RS	right side
sc	single crochet
sk	skip
st(s)	stitch(es)
V-st	(1 dc, ch 2, 1 dc) worked in same st or ch sp
WS	wrong side

ADDITIONAL STITCHES

DOUBLE TREBLE CROCHET (DTR)

Yarn over hook three times, insert hook into next stitch or fith chain, yarn over and pull through (yarn over and pull through two loops on hook) four times.

CLUSTER2 (CL2)

Yarn over hook, insert hook into next stitch, yarn over and pull through, yarn over and pull through two loops on the hook, yarn over and insert hook into same stitch, yarn over and pull through (four loops on hook), yarn over and pull through two loops (three loops on hook), yarn over and pull through all loops on hook.

BLANKET

Make 347 sts using the long tail foundation method.

ROW 1

Ch 5, 1 V-st in first st of long tail foundation, *ch 2, sk 2 sts, 1 sc in next st, ch 2, sk 2 sts, 1 dc in each of next 20 sts, ch 2, sk 2 sts, 1 sc in next st, ch 2, sk 2 sts**, 1 dc in each of next 75 sts*, rep from * twice more, then from * to ** once, 1 V-st in ch sp of V-st (347 sts).

ROW 2

Ch 5, 1 V-st in ch sp of V-st, *ch 5, sk [ch 2, 1 sc, ch 2], 1 dc in each of next 9 sts, ch 2, sk 2 sts, 1 dc in each of next 9 sts, ch 5, sk [ch 2, 1 sc, ch 2]**, 1 dc in each of next 3 sts, 17 OSq, 1 CSq, 17 OSq, 1 dc in each of next 2 sts, rep from * twice more, then from * to ** once, 1 V-st in ch sp of V-st.

ROW 3

Ch 5, 1 V-st in ch sp of V-st, *ch 2, sk ch 2, 1 sc in next ch, ch 2, sk ch 2, 1 dc in each of next 7 sts, ch 3, sk 2 dc, 1 sc in next ch sp, ch 3, sk 2 dc, 1 dc in each of next 7 sts, ch 2, sk ch 2, 1 sc in next ch, ch 2, sk ch 2**, 1 dc in each of next 3 sts, 16 OSq, 1 CSq, 1 OSq, 1 CSq, 16 OSq, 1 dc in each of next 2 sts, rep from * twice more, then from * to ** once, 1 V-st in ch sp of V-st.

ROW 4

Ch 5, 1 V-st in ch sp of V-st, *ch 5, sk [ch 2, 1 sc, ch 2], 1 dc in each of next 5 sts, ch 3, sk 2 dc, 1 sc in next ch sp, ch 5, 1 sc in next ch sp, ch 3, sk 2 dc, 1 dc in each of next 5 sts, ch 5, sk [ch 2, 1 sc, ch 2]**, 1 dc in each of next 3 sts, 15 OSq, 1 CSq, ch 5, sk [cl2, 1 dc], 1 dtr in ch sp, ch 5, sk [1 dc, cl2], 1 dc in next st, 1 CSq, 15 OSq, 1 dc in each of next 2 sts, rep from * twice more, then from * to ** once, 1 V-st in ch sp of V-st.

ROW 5

Ch 5, 1 V-st in ch sp of V-st, *ch 2, sk ch 2, 1 sc in next ch, ch 2, sk ch 2, 1 dc in each of next 3 sts, ch 3, sk 2 dc, 1 sc in next ch sp, (ch 5, 1 sc in next ch sp) twice, ch 3, sk 2 dc, 1 dc in each of next 3 sts, ch 2, sk ch 2, 1 sc in next ch, ch 2, sk ch 2**, 1 dc in each of next 3 sts, 14 OSq, 1 CSq, ch 5, sk [cl2, 1 dc], 1 sc in next ch sp, 1 sc in dtr, 1 sc in next ch sp, ch 5, sk [1 dc, cl2], 1 dc in next st, 1 CSq, 14 OSq, 1 dc in each of next 2 sts, rep from * twice more, then from * to ** once, 1 V-st in ch sp of V-st.

ROW 6

Ch 5, 1 V-st in ch sp of V-st, *ch 5, sk [ch 2, 1 sc, ch 2], 1 dc in each of next 3 sts, 2 dc in ch sp, ch 3, 1 sc in next ch sp, ch 5, 1 sc in next ch sp, ch 3, 2 dc in next ch sp, 1 dc in each of next 3 sts, ch 5, sk [ch 2, 1 sc, ch 2]**, 1 dc in each of next 3 sts, 13 OSq, 1 CSq, ch 6, sk [cl2, 1 dc], 1 sc in next ch, 1 sc in each of next 3 sc, 1 sc in next ch, ch 6, sk [1 dc, cl2], 1 dc in next st, 1 CSq, 13 OSq, 1 dc in each of next 2 sts, rep from * twice more, then from * to ** once, 1 V-st in ch sp of V-st.

ROW 7

Ch 5, 1 V-st in ch sp of V-st, *ch 2, sk ch 2, 1 sc in next ch, ch 2, sk ch 2, 1 dc in each of next 5 sts, 2 dc in ch sp, ch 3, 1 sc in next ch sp, ch 3, 2 dc in next ch sp, 1 dc in each of next 5 sts, ch 2, sk ch 2, 1 sc in next ch, ch 2, sk ch 2**, 1 dc in each of next 3 sts, 12 OSq, 1 CSq, ch 7, sk [cl2, 1 dc], 1 sc in next ch, 1 sc in each of next 5 sc, 1 sc in next ch, ch 7, sk [1 dc, cl2], 1 dc in next st, 1 CSq, 12 OSq, 1 dc in each of next 2 sts, rep from * twice more, then from * to ** once, 1 V-st in ch sp of V-st.

ROW 8

Ch 5, 1 V-st in ch sp of V-st, *ch 5, sk [ch 2, 1 sc, ch 2], 1 dc in each of next 7 sts, 2 dc in ch sp, ch 2, 2 dc in next ch sp, 1 dc in each of next 7 sts, ch 5, sk [ch 2, 1 sc, ch 2]**, 1 dc in each of next 3 sts, 11 OSq, 1 CSq, 1 OSq, [cl2, 1 dc] in ch sp, ch 6, sk 1 sc, 1 sc in each of next 5 sc, ch 6, sk 1 sc, [1 dc, cl2] in ch sp, 1 dc in next st, 1 OSq, 1 CSq, 11 OSq, 1 dc in each of next 2 sts, rep from * twice more, then from * to ** once, 1 V-st in ch sp of V-st.

ROW 9

Ch 5, 1 V-st in ch sp of V-st, *ch 2, sk ch 2, 1 sc in next ch, ch 2, sk ch 2, 1 dc in each of next 7 sts, ch 3, sk 2 dc, 1 sc in next ch sp, ch 3, sk 2 dc, 1 dc in each of next 7 sts, ch 2, sk ch 2, 1 sc in next ch, ch 2, sk ch 2**, 1 dc in each of next 3 sts, 10 OSq, 1 CSq, ch 5, sk [cl2, 1 dc], 1 dtr in ch sp, ch 5, sk [1 dc, cl2], 1 dc in next st, [cl2, 1 dc] in ch sp, ch 5, sk 1 sc, 1 sc in each of next 3 sc, sk 1 sc, ch 5, [1 dc, cl2] in ch sp, 1 dc in next st, ch 5, sk [cl2, 1 dc], 1 dtr in ch sp, ch 5, sk [1 dc, cl2], 1 dc in next st, 1 CSq, 10 OSq, 1 dc in each of next 2 sts, rep from * twice more, then from * to ** once, 1 V-st in ch sp of V-st.

ROW 10

Ch 5, 1 V-st in ch sp of V-st, *ch 5, sk [ch 2, 1 sc, ch 2], 1 dc in each of next 5 sts, ch 3, sk 2 dc, 1 sc in next ch sp, ch 5, 1 sc in next ch sp, ch 3, sk 2 dc, 1 dc in each of next 5 sts, ch 5, sk [ch 2, 1 sc, ch 2]**, 1 dc in each of next 3 sts, 9 OSq, 1 CSq, ch 5, sk [cl2, 1 dc], 1 sc in next ch sp, 1 sc in dtr, 1 sc in next ch sp, ch 5, sk [1 dc, cl2], 1 dc in next st, [cl2, 1 dc] in ch sp, ch 3, 1 dtr in middle sc, ch 3, [1 dc, cl2] in ch sp, 1 dc in next st, ch 5, 1 sc in next ch sp, 1 sc in dtr, 1 sc in next ch sp, ch 5, sk [1 dc, cl2], 1 dc in next st, 1 CSq, 9 OSq, 1 dc in each of next 2 sts, rep from * twice more, then from * to ** once, 1 V-st in ch sp of V-st.

ROW 11

Ch 5, 1 V-st in ch sp of V-st, *ch 2, sk ch 2, 1 sc in next ch, ch 2, sk ch 2, 1 dc in each of next 3 sts, ch 3, sk 2 dc, 1 sc in next ch sp, (ch 5, 1 sc in next ch sp) twice, ch 3, sk 2 dc, 1 dc in each of next 3 sts, ch 2, sk ch 2, 1 sc in next ch, ch 2, sk ch 2**, 1 dc in each of next 3 sts, 8 OSq, 1 CSq, ch 6, sk [cl2, 1 dc], 1 sc in next ch sp, 1 sc in each of next 3 sc, 1 sc in next ch sp, ch 6, sk [1 dc, cl2], 1 dc in next st, [cl2, 1 dc] in ch sp, ch 1, sk 1 dtr, [1 dc, cl2] in next ch sp, 1 dc in next st, ch 6, sk [cl2, 1 dc], 1 sc in next ch sp, 1 sc in each of next 3 sc, 1 sc in next ch sp, ch 6, sk [1 dc, cl2], 1 dc in next st, 1 CSq, 8 OSq, 1 dc in each of next 2 sts, rep from * twice more, then from * to ** once, 1 V-st in ch sp of V-st.

ROW 12

Ch 5, 1 V-st in ch sp of V-st, *ch 5, sk [ch 2, 1 sc, ch 2], 1 dc in each of next 3 sts, 2 dc in ch sp, ch 3, 1 sc in next ch sp, ch 5, 1 sc in next ch sp, ch 3, 2 dc in next ch sp, 1 dc in each of next 3 sts, ch 5, sk [ch 2, 1 sc, ch 2]**, 1 dc in each of next 3 sts, 7 OSq, 1 CSq, ch 7, sk [cl2, 1 dc], 1 sc in next ch sp, 1 sc in each of next 5 sc, 1 sc in next ch sp, ch 7, sk [1 dc, cl2], 1 dc in next st, 1 CSq, ch 7, sk [cl2, 1 dc], 1 sc in next ch sp, 1 sc in each of next 5 sc, 1 sc in next ch sp, ch 7, sk [1 dc, cl2], 1 dc in next st, 1 CSq, 7 OSq, 1 dc in each of next 2 sts, rep from * twice more, then from * to ** once, 1 V-st in ch sp of V-st.

ROW 13

Ch 5, 1 V-st in ch sp of V-st, *ch 2, sk ch 2, 1 sc in next ch, ch 2, sk ch 2, 1 dc in each of next 5 sts, 2 dc in ch sp, ch 3, 1 sc in next ch sp, ch 3, 2 dc in next ch sp, 1 dc in each of next 5 sts, ch 2, sk ch 2, 1 sc in next ch, ch 2, sk ch 2**, 1 dc in each of next 3 sts, 6 OSq, 1 CSq, 1 OSq, [cl2, 1 dc] in ch sp, ch 6, sk 1 sc, 1 sc in each of next 5 sc, ch 6, sk 1 sc, [1 dc, cl2] in ch sp, 1 dc in next st, 1 OSq, [cl2, 1 dc] in ch sp, ch 6, sk 1 sc, 1 sc in each of next 5 sc, ch 6, sk 1 sc, [1 dc, cl2] in ch sp, 1 dc in next st, 1 OSq, 1 CSq, 6 OSq, 1 dc in each of next 2 sts, rep from * twice more, then from * to ** once, 1 V-st in ch sp of V-st.

ROW 14

Ch 5, 1 V-st in ch sp of V-st, *ch 5, sk [ch 2, 1 sc, ch 2], 1 dc in each of next 7 sts, 2 dc in ch sp, ch 2, 2 dc in next ch sp, 1 dc in each of next 7 sts, ch 5, sk [ch 2, 1 sc, ch 2]**, 1 dc in each of next 3 sts, 5 OSq, 1 CSq, ch 5, sk [cl2, 1 dc], 1 dtr in ch sp, ch 5, sk [1 dc, cl2], 1 dc in next st, [cl2, 1 dc] in ch sp, ch 5, sk 1 sc, 1 sc in each of next 3 sc, ch 5, sk 1 sc, [1 dc, cl2] in ch sp, 1 dc in next st, 3 OSq, [cl2, 1 dc] in ch sp, ch 5, sk 1 sc, 1 sc in each of next 3 sc, ch 5, sk 1 sc, [1 dc, cl2] in ch sp, 1 dc in next st, ch 5, sk [cl2, 1 dc], 1 dtr in ch sp, ch 5, sk [1 dc, cl2], 1 dc in next st, 1 CSq, 5 OSq, 1 dc in each of next 2 sts, rep from * twice more, then from * to ** once, 1 V-st in ch sp of V-st.

⟶

ROW 15

Ch 5, 1 V-st in ch sp of V-st, *ch 2, sk ch 2, 1 sc in next ch, ch 2, sk ch 2, 1 dc in each of next 7 sts, ch 3, sk 2 dc, 1 sc in next ch sp, ch 3, sk 2 dc, 1 dc in each of next 7 sts, ch 2, sk ch 2, 1 sc in next ch, ch 2, sk ch 2**, 1 dc in each of next 3 sts, 4 OSq, 1 CSq, ch 5, sk [cl2, 1 dc], 1 sc in next ch sp, 1 sc in dtr, 1 sc in next ch sp, ch 5, sk [1 dc, cl2], 1 dc in next st, [cl2, 1 dc] in ch sp, ch 3, 1 dtr in middle sc, ch 3, [1 dc, cl2] in ch sp, 1 dc in next st, 5 OSq, [cl2, 1 dc] in ch sp, ch 3, 1 dtr in middle sc, ch 3, [1 dc, cl2] in ch sp, 1 dc in next st, ch 5, sk [cl2, 1 dc], 1 sc in next ch sp, 1 sc in dtr, 1 sc in next ch sp, ch 5, sk [1 dc, cl2], 1 dc in next st, 1 CSq, 4 OSq, 1 dc in each of next 2 sts, rep from * twice more, then from * to ** once, 1 V-st in ch sp of V-st.

ROW 16

Ch 5, 1 V-st in ch sp of V-st, *ch 5, sk [ch 2, 1 sc, ch 2], 1 dc in each of next 5 sts, ch 3, sk 2 dc, 1 sc in next ch sp, ch 5, 1 sc in next ch sp, ch 3, sk 2 dc, 1 dc in each of next 5 sts, ch 5, sk [ch 2, 1 sc, ch 2]**, 1 dc in each of next 3 sts, 3 OSq, 1 CSq, ch 6, sk [cl2, 1 dc], 1 sc in next ch sp, 1 sc in each of next 3 sc, 1 sc in next ch sp, ch 6, sk [1 dc, cl2], 1 dc in next st, [cl2, 1 dc] in ch sp, ch 1, sk 1 dtr, [1 dc, cl2] in next ch sp, 1 dc in next st, 7 OSq, [cl2, 1 dc] in ch sp, ch 1, sk 1 dtr, [1 dc, cl2] in next ch sp, 1 dc in next st, ch 6, sk [cl2, 1 dc], 1 sc in next ch sp, 1 sc in each of next 3 sc, 1 sc in next ch sp, ch 6, sk [1 dc, cl2], 1 dc in next st, 1 CSq, 3 OSq, 1 dc in each of next 2 sts, rep from * twice more, then from * to ** once, 1 V-st in ch sp of V-st.

ROW 17

Ch 5, 1 V-st in ch sp of V-st, *ch 2, sk ch 2, 1 sc in next ch, ch 2, sk ch 2, 1 dc in each of next 3 sts, ch 3, sk 2 dc, 1 sc in next ch sp, (ch 5, 1 sc in next ch sp) twice, ch 3, sk 2 dc, 1 dc in each of next 3 sts, ch 2, sk ch 2, 1 sc in next ch, ch 2, sk ch 2**, 1 dc in each of next 3 sts, 2 OSq, 1 CSq, ch 7, sk [cl2, 1 dc], 1 sc in next ch sp, 1 sc in each of next 5 sc, 1 sc in next ch sp, ch 7, sk [1 dc, cl2], 1 dc in next st, 1 CSq, 9 OSq, 1 CSq, ch 7, sk [cl2, 1 dc], 1 sc in next ch sp, 1 sc in each of next 5 sc, 1 sc in next ch sp, ch 7, sk [1 dc, cl2], 1 dc in next st, 1 CSq, 2 OSq, 1 dc in each of next 2 sts, rep from * twice more, then from * to ** once, 1 V-st in ch sp of V-st.

ROW 18

Ch 5, 1 V-st in ch sp of V-st, *ch 5, sk [ch 2, 1 sc, ch 2], 1 dc in each of next 3 sts, 2 dc in ch sp, ch 3, 1 sc in next ch sp, ch 5, 1 sc in next ch sp, ch 3, 2 dc in next ch sp, 1 dc in each of next 3 sts, ch 5, sk [ch 2, 1 sc, ch 2]**, 1 dc in each of next 3 sts, 3 OSq, [cl2, 1 dc] in ch sp, ch 6, sk 1 sc, 1 sc in each of next 5 sc, ch 6, sk 1 sc, [1 dc, cl2] in ch sp, 1 dc in next st, 1 OSq, 1 CSq, 7 OSq, 1 CSq, 1 OSq, [cl2, 1 dc] in ch sp, ch 6, sk 1 sc, 1 sc in each of next 5 sc, ch 6, sk 1 sc, [1 dc, cl2] in ch sp, 1 dc in next st, 3 OSq, 1 dc in each of next 2 sts, rep from * twice more, then from * to ** once, 1 V-st in ch sp of V-st.

ROW 19

Ch 5, 1 V-st in ch sp of V-st, *ch 2, sk ch 2, 1 sc in next ch, ch 2, sk ch 2, 1 dc in each of next 5 sts, 2 dc in ch sp, ch 3, 1 sc in next ch sp, ch 3, 2 dc in next ch sp, 1 dc in each of next 5 sts, ch 2, sk ch 2, 1 sc in next ch, ch 2, sk ch 2**, 1 dc in each of next 3 sts, 4 OSq, [cl2, 1 dc] in ch sp, ch 5, sk 1 sc, 1 sc in each of next 3 sc, ch 5, sk 1 sc, [1 dc, cl2] in ch sp, 1 dc in next st, ch 5, sk [cl2, 1 dc], 1 dtr in ch sp, ch 5, sk [1 dc, cl2], 1 dc in next st, 1 CSq, 5 OSq, 1 CSq, ch 5, sk [cl2, 1 dc], 1 dtr in ch sp, ch 5, sk [1 dc, cl2], 1 dc in next st, [cl2, 1 dc] in ch sp, ch 5, sk 1 sc, 1 sc in each of next 3 sc, ch 5, sk 1 sc, [1 dc, cl2] in ch sp, 1 dc in next st, 4 OSq, 1 dc in each of next 2 sts, rep from * twice more, then from * to ** once, 1 V-st in ch sp of V-st.

ROW 20

Ch 5, 1 V-st in ch sp of V-st, *ch 5, sk [ch 2, 1 sc, ch 2], 1 dc in each of next 7 sts, 2 dc in ch sp, ch 2, 2 dc in next ch sp, 1 dc in each of next 7 sts, ch 5, sk [ch 2, 1 sc, ch 2]**, 1 dc in each of next 3 sts, 5 OSq, [cl2, 1 dc] in ch sp, ch 3, 1 dtr in middle sc, ch 3, [1 dc, cl2] in ch sp, 1 dc in next st, ch 5, sk [cl2, 1 dc], 1 sc in next ch sp, 1 sc in dtr, 1 sc in next ch sp, ch 5, sk [1 dc, cl2], 1 dc in next st, 1 CSq, 3 OSq, 1 CSq, ch 5, sk [cl2, 1 dc], 1 sc in next ch sp, 1 sc in dtr, 1 sc in next ch sp, ch 5, sk [1 dc, cl2], 1 dc in next st, [cl2, 1 dc] in ch sp, ch 3, 1 dtr in middle sc, ch 3, [1 dc, cl2] in ch sp, 1 dc in next st, 5 OSq, 1 dc in each of next 2 sts, rep from * twice more, then from * to ** once, 1 V-st in ch sp of V-st.

ROW 21

Ch 5, 1 V-st in ch sp of V-st, *ch 2, sk ch 2, 1 sc in next ch, ch 2, sk ch 2, 1 dc in each of next 7 sts, ch 3, sk 2 dc, 1 sc in next ch sp, ch 3, sk 2 dc, 1 dc in each of next 7 sts, ch 2, sk ch 2, 1 sc in next ch, ch 2, sk ch 2**, 1 dc in each of next 3 sts, 6 OSq, [cl2, 1 dc] in ch sp, ch 1, [1 dc, cl2] in next ch sp, 1 dc in next st, ch 6, sk [cl2, 1 dc], 1 sc in next ch sp, 1 sc in each of next 3 sc, 1 sc in next ch sp, ch 6, sk [1 dc, cl2], 1 dc in next st, 1 CSq, 1 OSq, 1 CSq, ch 6, sk [cl2, 1 dc], 1 sc in next ch sp, 1 sc in each of next 3 sc, 1 sc in next ch sp, ch 6, sk [1 dc, cl2], 1 dc in next st, [cl2, 1 dc] in ch sp, ch 1, [1 dc, cl2] in next ch sp, 1 dc in next st, 6 OSq, 1 dc in each of next 2 sts, rep from * twice more, then from * to ** once, 1 V-st in ch sp of V-st.

ROW 22

Ch 5, 1 V-st in ch sp of V-st, *ch 5, sk [ch 2, 1 sc, ch 2], 1 dc in each of next 5 sts, ch 3, sk 2 dc, 1 sc in next ch sp, ch 5, 1 sc in next ch sp, ch 3, sk 2 dc, 1 dc in each of next 5 sts, ch 5, sk [ch 2, 1 sc, ch 2]**, 1 dc in each of next 3 sts, 7 OSq, 1 CSq, ch 7, sk [cl2, 1 dc], 1 sc in next ch sp, 1 sc in each of next 5 sc, 1 sc in next ch sp, ch 7, sk [1 dc, cl2], 1 dc in next st, 1 CSq, ch 7, sk [cl2, 1 dc], 1 sc in next ch sp, 1 sc in each of next 5 sc, 1 sc in next ch sp, ch 7, sk [1 dc, cl2], 1 dc in next st, 1 CSq, 7 OSq, 1 dc in each of next 2 sts, rep from * twice more, then from * to ** once, 1 V-st in ch sp of V-st.

ROW 23

Ch 5, 1 V-st in ch sp of V-st, *ch 2, sk ch 2, 1 sc in next ch, ch 2, sk ch 2, 1 dc in each of next 3 sts, ch 3, sk 2 dc, 1 sc in next ch sp, (ch 5, 1 sc in next ch sp) twice, ch 3, sk 2 dc, 1 dc in each of next 3 sts, ch 2, sk ch 2, 1 sc in next ch, ch 2, sk ch 2**, 1 dc in each of next 3 sts, 8 OSq, [cl2, 1 dc] in ch sp, ch 6, sk 1 sc, 1 sc in each of next 5 sc, ch 6, sk 1 sc, [1 dc, cl2] in ch sp, 1 dc in next st, 1 OSq, [cl2, 1 dc] in ch sp, ch 6, sk 1 sc, 1 sc in each of next 5 sc, ch 6, sk 1 sc, [1 dc, cl2] in ch sp, 1 dc in next st, 8 OSq, 1 dc in each of next 2 sts, rep from * twice more, then from * to ** once, 1 V-st in ch sp of V-st.

ROW 24

Ch 5, 1 V-st in ch sp of V-st, *ch 5, sk [ch 2, 1 sc, ch 2], 1 dc in each of next 3 sts, 2 dc in ch sp, ch 3, 1 sc in next ch sp, ch 5, 1 sc in next ch sp, ch 3, 2 dc in next ch sp, 1 dc in each of next 3 sts, ch 5, sk [ch 2, 1 sc, ch 2]**, 1 dc in each of next 3 sts, 9 OSq, [cl2, 1 dc] in ch sp, ch 5, sk 1 sc, 1 sc in each of next 3 sc, ch 5, sk 1 sc, [1 dc, cl2] in ch sp, 1 dc in next st, ch 5, sk [cl2, 1 dc], 1 dtr in ch sp, ch 5, sk [1 dc, cl2], 1 dc in next st, [cl2, 1 dc] in ch sp, ch 5, sk 1 sc, 1 sc in each of next 3 sc, ch 5, sk 1 sc,[1 dc, cl2] in ch sp, 1 dc in next st, 9 OSq, 1 dc in each of next 2 sts, rep from * twice more, then from * to ** once, 1 V-st in ch sp of V-st.

ROW 25

Ch 5, 1 V-st in ch sp of V-st, *ch 2, sk ch 2, 1 sc in next ch, ch 2, sk ch 2, 1 dc in each of next 5 sts, 2 dc in ch sp, ch 3, 1 sc in next ch sp, ch 3, 2 dc in next ch sp, 1 dc in each of next 5 sts, ch 2, sk ch 2, 1 sc in next ch, ch 2, sk ch 2**, 1 dc in each of next 3 sts, 10 OSq, [cl2, 1 dc] in ch sp, ch 3, 1 dtr in middle sc, ch 3, [1 dc, cl2] in ch sp, 1 dc in next st, ch 5, sk [cl2, 1 dc], 1 sc in ch sp, 1 sc in dtr, 1 sc in next ch sp, ch 5, sk [1 dc, cl2], 1 dc in st, [cl2, 1 dc] in ch sp, ch 3, 1 dtr in middle sc, ch 3, [1 dc, cl2] in next ch sp, 1 dc in next st, 10 OSq, 1 dc in each of next 2 sts, rep from * twice more, then from * to ** once, 1 V-st in ch sp of V-st.

→

ROW 26

Ch 5, 1 V-st in ch sp of V-st, *ch 5, sk [ch 2, 1 sc, ch 2], 1 dc in each of next 7 sts, 2 dc in ch sp, ch 2, 2 dc in next ch sp, 1 dc in each of next 7 sts, ch 5, sk [ch 2, 1 sc, ch 2]**, 1 dc in each of next 3 sts, 11 OSq, [cl2, 1 dc] in ch sp, ch 1, sk 1 dtr, [1 dc, cl2] in next ch sp, 1 dc in next st, ch 6, sk [cl2, 1 dc], 1 sc in next ch sp, 1 sc in each of next 3 sc, 1 sc in next ch sp, ch 6, sk [1 dc, cl2], 1 dc in next st, [cl2, 1 dc] in ch sp, ch 1, sk 1 dtr, [1 dc, cl2] in next ch sp, 1 dc in next st, 11 OSq, 1 dc in each of next 2 sts, rep from * twice more, then from * to ** once, 1 V-st in ch sp of V-st.

ROW 27

Ch 5, 1 V-st in ch sp of V-st, *ch 2, sk ch 2, 1 sc in next ch, ch 2, sk ch 2, 1 dc in each of next 7 sts, ch 3, sk 2 dc, 1 sc in next ch sp, ch 3, sk 2 dc, 1 dc in each of next 7 sts, ch 2, sk ch 2, 1 sc in next ch, ch 2, sk ch 2**, 1 dc in each of next 3 sts, 12 OSq, 1 CSq, ch 7, sk [cl2, 1 dc], 1 sc in next ch sp, 1 sc in each of next 5 sc, 1 sc in next ch sp, ch 7, sk [1 dc, cl2], 1 dc in next st, 1 CSq, 12 OSq, 1 dc in each of next 2 sts, rep from * twice more, then from * to ** once, 1 V-st in ch sp of V-st.

ROW 28

Ch 5, 1 V-st in ch sp of V-st, *ch 5, sk [ch 2, 1 sc, ch 2], 1 dc in each of next 5 sts, ch 3, sk 2 dc, 1 sc in next ch sp, ch 5, 1 sc in next ch sp, ch 3, sk 2 dc, 1 dc in each of next 5 sts, ch 5, sk [ch 2, 1 sc, ch 2]**, 1 dc in each of next 3 sts, 13 OSq, [cl2, 1 dc] in ch sp, ch 6, sk 1 sc, 1 sc in each of next 5 sc, ch 6, sk 1 sc, [1 dc, cl2] in ch sp, 1 dc in next st, 13 OSq, 1 dc in each of next 2 sts, rep from * twice more, then from * to ** once, 1 V-st in ch sp of V-st.

ROW 29

Ch 5, 1 V-st in ch sp of V-st, *ch 2, sk ch 2, 1 sc in next ch, ch 2, sk ch 2, 1 dc in each of next 3 sts, ch 3, sk 2 dc, 1 sc in next ch sp, (ch 5, 1 sc in next ch sp) twice, ch 3, sk 2 dc, 1 dc in each of next 3 sts, ch 2, sk ch 2, 1 sc in next ch, ch 2, sk ch 2**, 1 dc in each of next 3 sts, 14 OSq, [cl2, 1 dc] in ch sp, ch 5, sk 1 sc, 1 sc in each of next 3 sc, ch 5, sk 1 sc, [1 dc, cl2] in ch sp, 1 dc in next st, 14 OSq, 1 dc in each of next 2 sts, rep from * twice more, then from * to ** once, 1 V-st in ch sp of V-st.

ROW 30

Ch 5, 1 V-st in ch sp of V-st, *ch 5, sk [ch 2, 1 sc, ch 2], 1 dc in each of next 3 sts, 2 dc in ch sp, ch 3, 1 sc in next ch sp, ch 5, 1 sc in next ch sp, ch 3, 2 dc in next ch sp, 1 dc in each of next 3 sts, ch 5, sk [ch 2, 1 sc, ch 2]**, 1 dc in each of next 3 sts, 15 OSq, [cl2, 1 dc] in ch sp, ch 3, 1 dtr in middle sc, ch 3, [1 dc, cl2] in ch sp, 1 dc in next st, 15 OSq, 1 dc in each of next 2 sts, rep from * twice more, then from * to ** once, 1 V-st in ch sp of V-st.

ROW 31

Ch 5, 1 V-st in ch sp of V-st, *ch 2, sk ch 2, 1 sc in next ch, ch 2, sk ch 2, 1 dc in each of next 5 sts, 2 dc in ch sp, ch 3, 1 sc in next ch sp, ch 3, 2 dc in next ch sp, 1 dc in each of next 5 sts, ch 2, sk ch 2, 1 sc in next ch, ch 2, sk ch 2**, 1 dc in each of next 3 sts, 16 OSq, [cl2, 1 dc] in ch sp, ch 1, sk 1 dtr, [1 dc, cl2] in ch sp, 1 dc in next st, 16 OSq, 1 dc in each of next 2 sts, rep from * twice more, then from * to ** once, 1 V-st in ch sp of V-st.

ROW 32

Ch 5, 1 V-st in ch sp of V-st, *ch 5, sk [ch 2, 1 sc, ch 2], 1 dc in each of next 7 sts, 2 dc in ch sp, ch 2, 2 dc in next ch sp, 1 dc in each of next 7 sts, ch 5, sk [ch 2, 1 sc, ch 2]**, 1 dc in each of next 3 sts, 17 OSq, 1 CSq, 17 OSq, 1 dc in each of next 2 sts, rep from * twice more, then from * to ** once, 1 V-st in ch sp of V-st.

Rep rows 3–32 until the blanket is the correct length.

LAST ROW

Ch 5, 1 V-st in the ch sp of the V-st, ch 2, sk ch 2, 1 sc in next ch, ch 2, sk ch 2, 1 dc in each st (dc, ch or cl) to last 5-ch sp, ch 2, sk ch 2, 1 sc in next ch, ch 2, sk ch 2, 1 V-st in ch sp of V-st.

Fasten off and weave in ends.

Last row
REPEAT
31
29
27
25
23
21
19
17
15
13
11
9
7
5
3
1
1
5
20
5
75
REPEAT
5
20
5
1
32
30
28
26
24
22
20
18
16
14
12
10
8
6
4
2

Timeless Illusions

With this nostalgic-looking throw, you can see something different every time. Some people identify flowers in the pattern, while some see leaves, and others find squares with flared points. A true illusion!

MATERIALS

14 balls of **Durable Cotton No. 6**
1–3-ply (lace weight) cotton yarn
(100g/3½oz/300m/328yd) in White (009)

TOOLS

3mm (US G-2/D-3, UK 11) crochet hook
Tapestry needle
Stitch markers

FINISHED SIZE

Approx. 150 × 205cm (59 × 81in)

DIFFICULTY LEVEL

Easy

PATTERN NOTES

The blanket is worked in rows, which means you will need to turn the work at the end of each row.

Each row starts with 2 ch. These chs are not listed separately and count as the first stitch.

STITCHES AND ABBREVIATIONS USED

ch	chain(s)
ch sp(s)	chain space(s)
dc	double crochet
PM	place marker
RS	right side
sk	skip
sl st	slip stitch
sp(s)	space(s)
st(s)	stitch(es)
WS	wrong side

KEY

– long tail foundation

– chain

– double crochet

BLANKET

Make 280 sts using the long tail foundation method.

ROW 1 (RS)
1 dc in each st (280 sts).

ROW 2 (WS)
1 dc in each st (280 sts).

ROW 3
1 dc in each of next 7 sts. *ch 4, sk 4 sts, 1 dc in each of next 24 sts, ch 4, sk 4 sts, 1 dc in each of next 7 sts, rep from * six more times.

ROW 4
*1 dc in each of next 7 sts, ch 8, sk 8 st, 1 dc in each of next 16 sts, ch 8, sk 8 sts, rep from * six more times, 1 dc in each of last 7 sts.

ROW 5
1 dc in each of next 7 sts, *2 dc in ch sp, ch 6, sk 6 sts, 1 dc in next st, (ch 4, sk 4 sts, 1 dc in next st) three times, ch 6, sk 6 sts, 2 dc in the ch sp, 1 dc in each of next 7 sts, rep from * six more times.

ROW 6
*1 dc in each of next 9 sts, ch 6, sk 6 sts, 1 dc in next st, (ch 4, sk 4 sts, 1 dc in next st) three times, ch 6, sk 6 sts, 1 dc in each of next 2 sts, rep from * six more times, 1 dc in each of last 7 sts.

ROW 7
1 dc in each of next 7 sts, *1 dc in each of next 2 sts, 2 dc in ch sp, (ch 4, sk 4 sts, 1 dc in next st) twice, 4 dc in the ch sp, 1 dc in next st, ch 4, sk 4 sts, 1 dc in next st, ch 4, sk 4 sts, 2 dc in ch sp, 1 dc in each of next 9 sts, rep from * six more times.

ROW 8
*1 dc in each of next 11 sts, (ch 4, sk 4 sts, 1 dc in next st, 4 dc in ch sp, 1 dc in next st) twice, ch 4, sk 4 sts, 1 dc in each of next 4 sts, rep from * six more times, 1 dc in each of last 7 sts.

ROW 9
1 dc in each of next 7 sts, *1 dc in each of next 4 sts, (ch 4, sk 4 sts, 1 dc in each of next 6 sts) twice, ch 4, sk 4 sts, 1 dc in each of next 11 sts, rep from * six more times.

ROW 10
*1 dc in each of next 11 sts, (ch 4, sk 4 sts, 1 dc in next st) twice, 4 dc in ch sp, 1 dc in next st, ch 4, sk 4 sts, 1 dc in next st, ch 4, sk 4 sts, 1 dc in each of next 4 sts, rep from * six more times, 1 dc in each of last 7 sts.

ROW 11
1 dc in each of next 7 sts, *1 dc in each of next 2 sts, ch 6, sk 6 sts, 1 dc in next st, (ch 4, sk 4 sts, 1 dc in next st) three times, ch 6, sk 6 sts, 1 dc in each of next 9 sts, rep from * six more times.

ROW 12
*1 dc in each of next 9 sts, ch 6, sk 6 sts, 1 dc in next st, (ch 4, sk 4 sts, 1 dc in next st) three times, ch 6, sk 6 sts, 1 dc in each of next 2 sts, rep from * six more times, 1 dc in each of last 7 sts.

ROW 13
1 dc in each of next 7 sts, *ch 8, sk 8 sts, 1 dc in next st, (4 dc in the ch sp, 1 dc in next st) three times, ch 8, sk 8 sts, 1 dc in each of next 7 sts, rep from * six more times.

ROW 14
*1 dc in each of next 7 sts, ch 4, sk 4 sts, 4 dc in ch sp, 1 dc in each of next 16 sts, 4 dc in ch sp, ch 4, sk 4 sts, rep from * six more times, 1 dc in each of last 7 sts.

ROW 15
1 dc in each of next 7 sts, *4 dc in ch sp, 1 dc in each of next 24 sts, 4 dc in ch sp, 1 dc in next st**, ch 5, sk 5 sts, 1 dc in next st, rep from * five more times, then from * to ** once, 1 dc in each of last 6 sts.

ROW 16
1 dc in each of next 39 sts, *1 dc in next st, ch 5, sk 5 sts, 1 dc in next 33 sts, rep from * five more times, 1 dc in each of last 7 sts.

ROW 17
1 dc in each of next 7 sts, *ch 4, sk 4 sts, 1 dc in each of next 24 sts, ch 4, sk 4 sts, 1 dc in next st**, 5 dc in ch sp, 1 dc in next st, rep from * five more times, then from * to ** once, 1 dc in each of last 6 sts.

ROWS 18–210
Rep rows 4–17 thirteen more times, then rows 4–14 once more.

ROWS 211 AND 212
1 dc in each st (rows 15a and 16a on chart).

Fasten off and weave in ends.

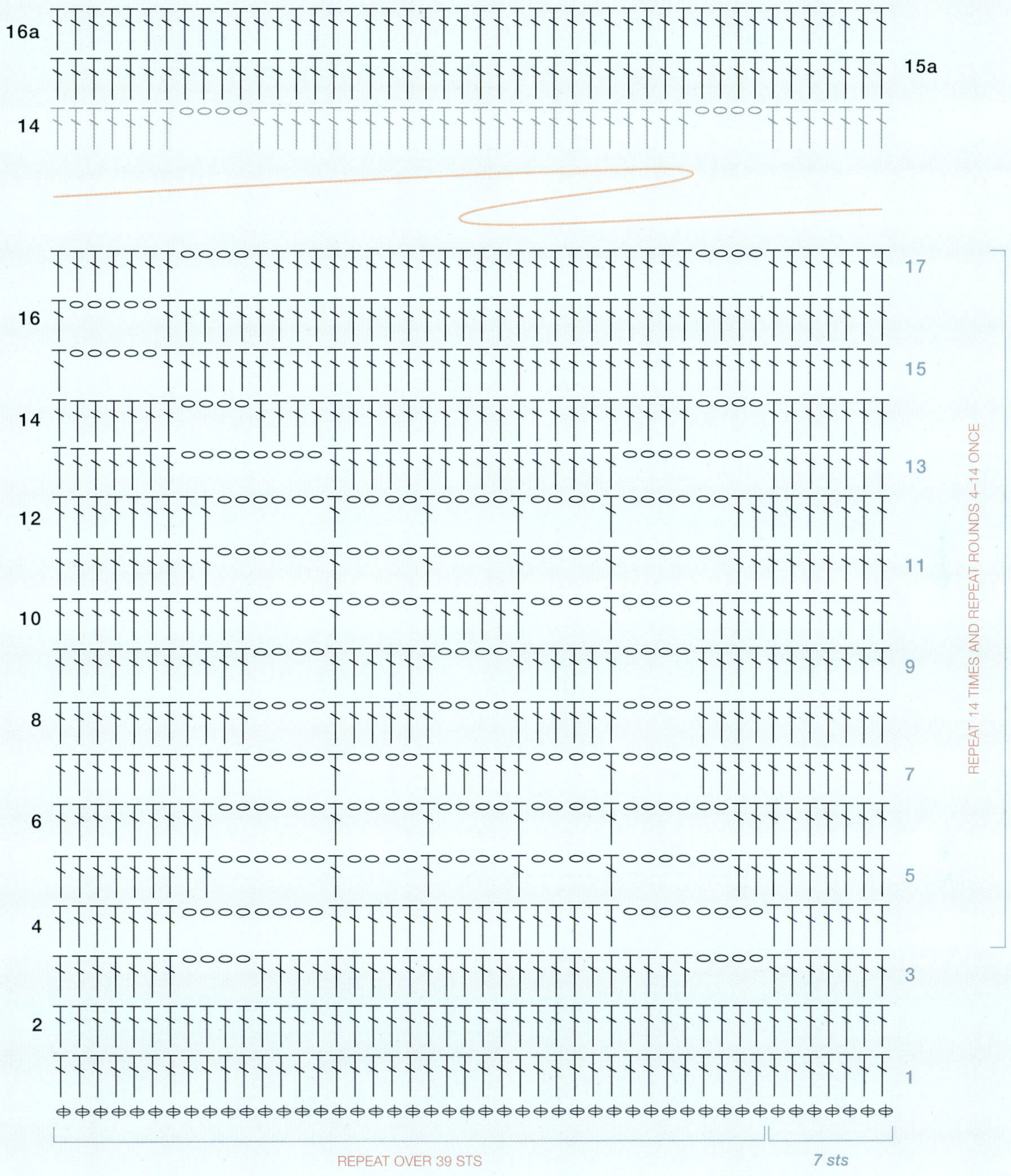

Pattern Repeat Chart

BORDER

Crochet the border in the round on the RS of the work.

NOTE

If the blanket starts to pull in, add an extra ch as necessary. You can also use a smaller hook if you notice that the edge starts to ripple or bulge.

ROUND 1

Join yarn in the upper right corner st, [1 dc, ch 3, 1 dc] in same st, *ch 4, sk 4 sts, 1 dc in next st, rep from * to last 4 sts of this side, ch 3, sk 3 sts, [1 dc, ch 3, 1 dc] in last st, turn to work along left side, **ch 4, sk posts of 2 dc, 1 dc in top of next dc, rep from ** to last 2 rows, ch 4, sk posts of 2 dc, [1 dc, ch 3, 1 dc] in bottom of last dc of this side, turn to work along bottom edge, ch 3, sk 3 sts, 1 dc in next st, ***ch 4, sk 4 sts, 1 dc in next st, rep from *** to last 5 sts on this side, ch 4, sk 4 sts, [1 dc, ch 3, 1 dc] in last st, turn to work right side, ****ch 4, sk post of 1 dc, 1 dc in top of next dc, rep from **** to last 2 rows, ch 4, sk post of 1 dc, join with sl st in first st.

ROUND 2

1 dc in first st, [ch 3, 1 dc in corner sp (PM in this st), ch 3], 1 dc in next st, continue in the same way working ch 4 above 4-ch sps, ch 3 above 3-ch sps, 1 dc into each dc and [ch 3, 1 dc (PM), ch 3] in each corner sp, join with sl st in first st.

ROUND 3

1 dc in first st, [3 dc in 3-ch sp, 3 dc in marked corner st (PM in centre st), 3 dc in next 3-ch sp] (corner made), work 1 dc in each st and ch, continue in same way around, join with a sl st in first st.

ROUND 4

1 dc in each st, 3 dc in each marked st, join with a sl st in first st.

Fasten off and weave in ends.

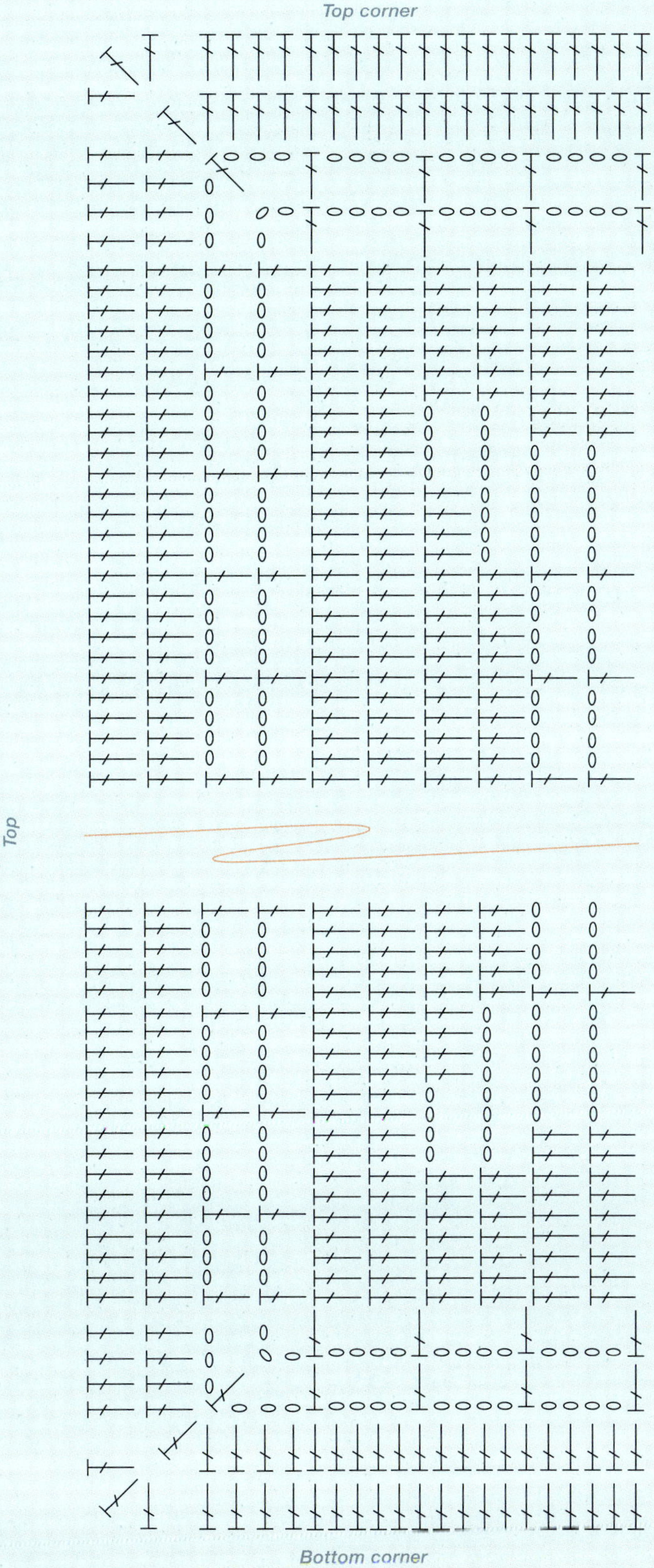

Border Chart

Winter White

The white of the yarn and the motifs in this throw perfectly represent snow, stars and snowflakes, embodying the spirit of winter.

MATERIALS

17 balls of **Durable Cotton No. 6**
1–3-ply (lace weight) cotton yarn
100g/3½oz/300m/328yd in White (009)

TOOLS

2.5mm (US 1/2, UK 13/12) crochet hook
Tapestry needle
Stitch markers

FINISHED SIZE

1 square
45 × 45cm (18 × 18in)

Blanket
Approx. 185 × 140cm (73 × 55in)

DIFFICULTY LEVEL

Medium

KEY

– *magic ring*
– *chain*
– *slip stitch*
– *single crochet*
– *half double crochet*
– *double crochet*
– *bobble stitch (tr 5 together worked into 1 stitch)*

PATTERN NOTES

The blanket is worked in rows, which means you will need to turn the work at the end of each row before beginning the next.

Each row starts with 2 ch. These chs count as the first stitch and are not detailed specifically in the instructions.

STITCHES AND ABBREVIATIONS USED

bo	bobble; tr 5 together in same stitch or space
ch	chain(s)
ch sp(s)	chain space(s)
dc	double crochet
hdc	half double crochet
RS	right side
sk	skip
sl st	slip stitch
sp(s)	space(s)
st(s)	stitch(es)
tr	treble crochet

ADDITIONAL STITCHES

TREBLE CROCHET (TR)

Yarn over hook twice, insert hook into next stitch or fifth chain from hook, yarn over; pull through; yarn over, pull through two loops, yarn over pull through two loops; yarn over pull through two loops.

BOBBLE STITCH (BO)

Yarn over hook twice, insert hook into next stitch, yarn over, pull through, (yarn over, pull through two loops on hook) twice, *yarn over twice, insert hook into same stitch (yarn over, pull through two loops on hook) twice, rep from * three more times (six loops on hook), yarn over and pull through all loops on hook.

SQUARE

(make 12)

Make a magic ring.

ROUND 1

(3 dc, ch 3) three times into ring, (3 dc, ch 1) into ring, join with 1 hdc in first st.

ROUND 2

2 dc in corner sp, *1 dc in each of next 3 sts, [2 dc, ch 3, 2 dc] in corner sp, rep from * twice more, 1 dc in each of next 3 sts, 2 dc in corner sp, ch 1, join with 1 hdc in first st.

ROUND 3

2 dc in corner sp, *1 dc in each of next 3 sts, bo in next st, 1 dc in each of next 3 sts, [2 dc**, ch 3, 2 dc] in corner sp, rep from * twice more, then from * to ** once, ch 1, join with 1 hdc in first st.

ROUND 4

2 dc in corner sp, *1 dc in each of next 3 sts, bo in next st, 1 dc in next st, ch 1, sk 1 st, 1 dc in next st, bo in next st, 1 dc in each of next 3 sts, [2 dc**, ch 3, 2 dc] in corner sp, rep from * twice more, then from * to ** once, ch 1, join with 1 hdc in first st.

ROUND 5

2 dc in corner sp, *1 dc in each of next 3 sts, bo in next st, (1 dc in next st, ch 1, sk 1 st) three times, 1 dc in next st, bo in next st, 1 dc in each of next 3 sts, [2 dc**, ch 3, 2 dc] in corner sp, rep from * twice more, then from * to ** once, ch 1, join with 1 hdc in first st.

ROUND 6

2 dc in corner sp, *1 dc in each of next 3 sts, bo in next st, (1 dc in next st, ch 1, sk 1 st) five times, 1 dc in next st, bo in next st, 1 dc in each of next 3 sts, [2 dc**, ch 3, 2 dc] in corner sp, rep from * twice more, then from * to ** once, ch 1, join with 1 hdc in first st.

ROUND 7

2 dc in corner sp, *1 dc in each of next 7 sts, bo in next st, (1 dc in next st, ch 1, sk 1 st) three times, 1 dc in next st, bo in next st, 1 dc in each of next 7 sts, [2 dc**, ch 3, 2 dc] in corner sp, rep from * twice more, then from * to ** once, ch 1, join with 1 hdc in first st.

ROUND 8

2 dc in corner sp, *1 dc in each of next 4 sts, bo in next st, 1 dc in each of next 6 sts, bo in next st, 1 dc in next st, ch 1, sk 1 st, 1 dc in next st, bo in next st, 1 dc in each of next 6 sts, bo in next st, 1 dc in each of next 4 sts, [2 dc**, ch 3, 2 dc] in corner sp, rep from * twice more, then from * to ** once, ch 1, join with 1 hdc in first st.

ROUND 9

2 dc in corner sp, *1 dc in each of next 4 sts, bo in next st, 1 dc in next st, ch 1, sk 1 st, 1 dc in next st, bo in next st, 1 dc in each of next 6 sts. bo in next st, 1 dc in each of next 6 sts, bo in next st, 1 dc in next st, ch 1, sk 1 st, 1 dc in next st, bo in next st, 1 dc in each of next 4 sts, [2 dc**, ch 3, 2 dc] in corner sp, rep from * twice more, then from * to ** once, ch 1, join with 1 hdc in first st.

ROUND 10

2 dc in corner sp, *1 dc in each of next 4 sts, bo in next st, (1 dc in next st, ch 1, sk 1 st) three times, 1 dc in next st, bo in next st, 1 dc in each of next 9 sts, bo in next st, (1 dc in next st, ch 1, sk 1 st) three times, 1 dc in next st, bo in next st, 1 dc in each of next 4 sts, [2 dc**, ch 3, 2 dc] in corner sp, rep from * twice more, then from * to ** once, ch 1, join with 1 hdc in first st.

ROUND 11

2 dc in corner sp, *1 dc in each of next 4 sts, bo in next st, (1 dc in next st, ch 1, sk 1 st) five times, 1 dc in next st, bo in next st, 1 dc in each of next 5 sts, bo in next st, (1 dc in next st, ch 1, sk 1 st) five times, 1 dc in next st, bo in next st, 1 dc in each of next 4 sts, [2 dc**, ch 3, 2 dc] in corner sp, rep from * twice more, then from * to ** once, ch 1, join with 1 hdc in first st.

ROUND 12

2 dc in corner sp, *1 dc in each of next 8 sts, bo in next st, (1 dc in next st, ch 1, sk 1 st) three times, 1 dc in next st, bo in next st, 1 dc in each of next 9 sts, bo in next st, (1 dc in next st, ch 1, sk 1 st) three times, 1 dc in next st, bo in next st, 1 dc in each of next 8 sts. [2 dc**, ch 3, 2 dc] in corner sp, rep from * twice more, then from * to ** once, ch 1, join with 1 hdc in first st.

ROUND 13

2 dc in corner sp, *1 dc in each of next 12 sts, bo in next st, 1 dc in next st, ch 1, sk 1 st, 1 dc in next st, bo in next st, 1 dc in each of next 13 sts, bo in next st, 1 dc in next st, ch 1, sk 1 st, 1 dc in next st, bo in next st, 1 dc in each of next 12 sts, [2 dc**, ch 3, 2 dc] in corner sp, rep from * twice more, then from * to ** once, ch 1, join with 1 hdc in first st.

ROUND 14

2 dc in corner sp, *1 dc in each of next 16 st, bo in next st, 1 dc in each of next 17 sts, bo in next st, 1 dc in each of next 16 sts. [2 dc**, ch 3, 2 dc] in corner sp, rep from * twice more, then from * to ** once, ch 1, join with 1 hdc in first st.

ROUND 15

2 dc in corner sp, *1 dc in each of next 55 sts, [2 dc**, ch 3, 2 dc] in corner sp, rep from * twice more, then from * to ** once, ch 1, join with 1 hdc in first st.

ROUND 16

2 dc in corner sp, *1 dc in each of next 59 st, [2 dc**, ch 3, 2 dc] in corner sp, rep from * twice more, then from * to ** once, ch 1, join with 1 hdc in first st.

ROUND 17

2 dc in corner sp, *(1 dc in next st, ch 1, sk 1 st) thirty-one times, 1 dc in next st, [2 dc**, ch 3, 2 dc] in corner sp, rep from * twice more, then from * to ** once, ch 1, join with 1 hdc in first st.

ROUND 18

2 dc in corner sp, *1 dc in each of next 67 sts, [2 dc**, ch 3, 2 dc] in corner sp, rep from * twice more, then from * to ** once, ch 1, join with 1 hdc in first st.

ROUND 19

2 dc in corner sp, *1 dc in each of next 6 sts, (bo in next st, 1 dc in each of next 3 sts) five times, (bo in next st, 1 dc in each of next 8 sts) twice, (bo in next st, 1 dc in each of next 3 sts) five times, bo in next st, 1 dc in each of next 6 sts, [2 dc**, ch 3, 2 dc] in the corner sp, rep from * twice more, then from * to ** once, ch 1, join with 1 hdc in first st.

ROUND 20

2 dc in corner sp, *1 dc in each of next 6 sts, bo in next st, (1 dc in next st, ch 1, sk 1 st) nine times, 1 dc in next st, bo in next st, 1 dc in each of next 8 sts, bo in next st, 1 dc in next st, ch 1, sk 1 st, 1 dc in next st, bo in next st, 1 dc in each of next 8 sts, bo in next st, (1 dc in next st, ch 1, sk 1 st) nine times, 1 dc in next st, bo in next st, 1 dc in each of next 6 sts, [2 dc**, ch 3, 2 dc] in the corner sp, rep from * twice more, then from * to ** once, ch 1, join with 1 hdc in first st.

ROUND 21

2 dc in corner sp, *1 dc in each of next 6 sts, bo in next st, (1 dc in next st, ch 1, sk 1 st) nine times, 1 dc in next st, bo in next st, 1 dc in each of next 8 sts, bo in next st, (1 dc in next st, ch 1, sk 1 st) three times, 1 dc in next st, bo in next st, 1 dc in each of next 8 sts, bo in next st, (1 dc in next st, ch 1, sk 1 st) nine times, 1 dc in next st, bo in next st, 1 dc in each of next 6 sts, [2 dc**, ch 3, 2 dc] in the corner sp, rep from * twice more, then from * to ** once, ch 1, join with 1 hdc in first st.

ROUND 22

2 dc in corner sp, *1 dc in each of next 6 sts, bo in next st, (1 dc in next st, ch 1, sk 1 st) nine times, 1 dc in next st, bo in next st, 1 dc in each of next 12 sts, bo in next st, 1 dc in next st, ch 1, sk 1 st, 1 dc in next st, bo in next st, 1 dc in each of next 12 sts, bo in next st, (1 dc in next st, ch 1, sk 1 st) nine times, 1 dc in next st, bo in next st, 1 dc in each of next 6 sts, [2 dc**, ch 3, 2 dc] in the corner sp, rep from * twice more, then from * to ** once, ch 1, join with 1 hdc in first st.

ROUND 23

2 dc in corner sp, *1 dc in each of next 6 sts, (bo in next st, 1 dc in each of next 3 sts) five times, (bo in next st, 1 dc in each of next 16 sts) twice, (bo in next st, 1 dc in each of next 3 sts) five times, bo in next st, 1 dc in each of next 6 sts, [2 dc**, ch 3, 2 dc] in the corner sp, rep from * twice more, then from * to ** once, ch 1, join with 1 hdc in first st.

ROUND 24

2 dc in corner sp, *1 dc in each of next 91 sts, [2 dc**, ch 3, 2 dc] in corner sp, rep from * twice more, then from * to ** once, ch 3, 1 sl st in first st.

Fasten off and weave in ends.

JOINING

Join the squares RS together, in rows of four by three, using sc.

Start by joining squares in a row, then join the rows together.

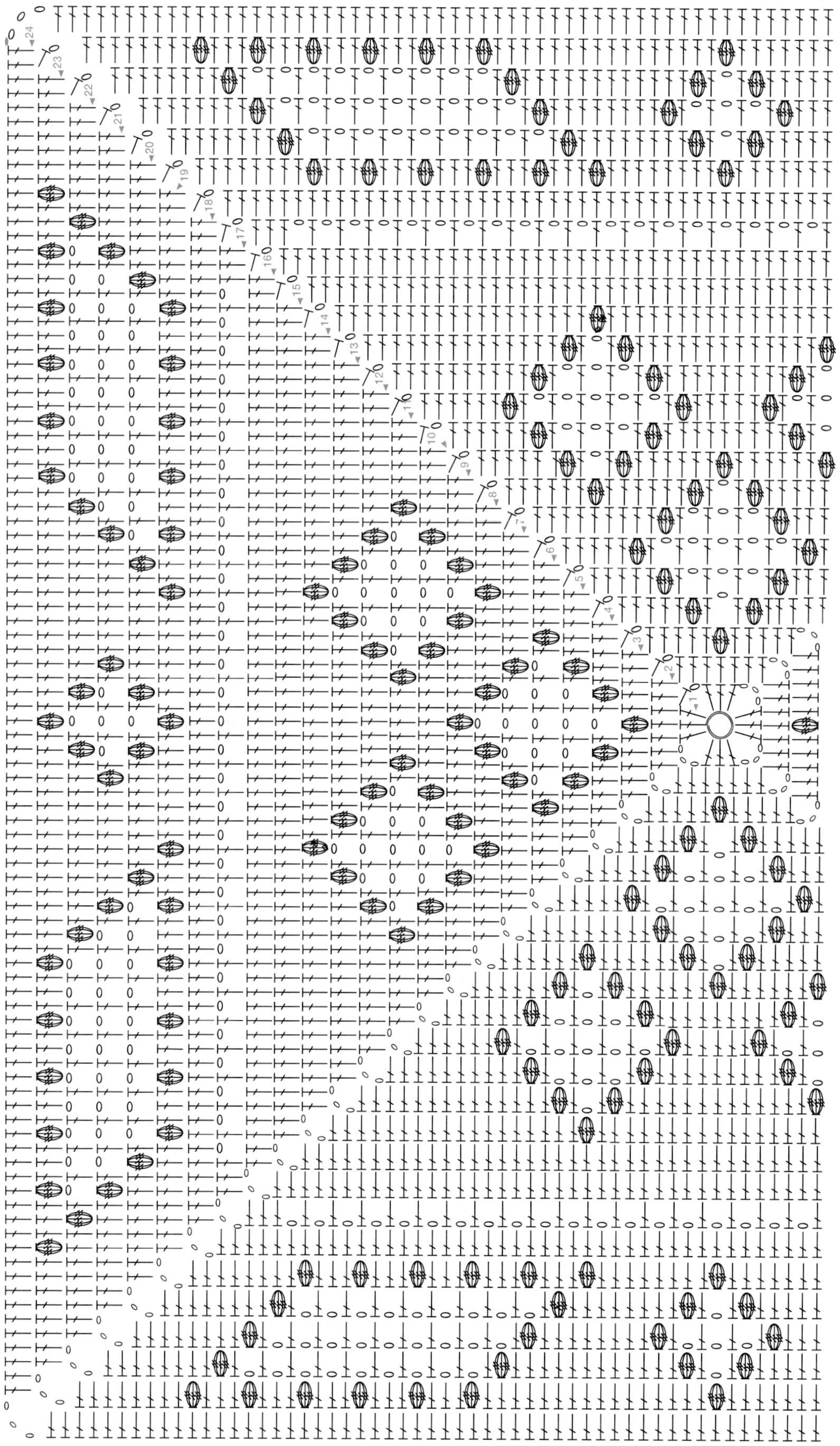

Square Chart Cross-section

BORDER

ROUND 1

Join yarn in a corner sp, 2 dc in corner sp, *1 dc in each st to where two squares join, 2 dc in first ch sp, 1 dc in seam, 2 dc in next ch sp, rep from * to last square, 1 dc in each st to corner, [2 dc, ch 3, 2 dc] in corner sp, continue in the same way around, in last corner sp work 2 dc, ch 1, join with 1 hdc in first st.

ROUND 2

2 dc in corner sp, 1 dc in first st, *ch 1, sk 1 st, 1 dc in next st, rep from * to end of this side, [2 dc, ch 3, 2 dc] in corner sp, continue in the same way around, in last corner sp work 2 dc, ch 1, join with 1 hdc in first st.

ROUND 3

2 dc in corner sp, 1 dc in each st and ch to end of this side, [2 dc, ch 3, 2 dc] in corner sp, continue in the same way around, in last corner sp work 2 dc, ch 1, join with 1 hdc in first st.

ROUND 4

2 dc in corner sp, 1 dc in each st to end of this side, [2 dc, ch 3, 2 dc] in corner sp, continue in the same way around, in last corner sp work 2 dc, ch 3, join with a sl st.

Fasten off and weave in ends.

Border Chart

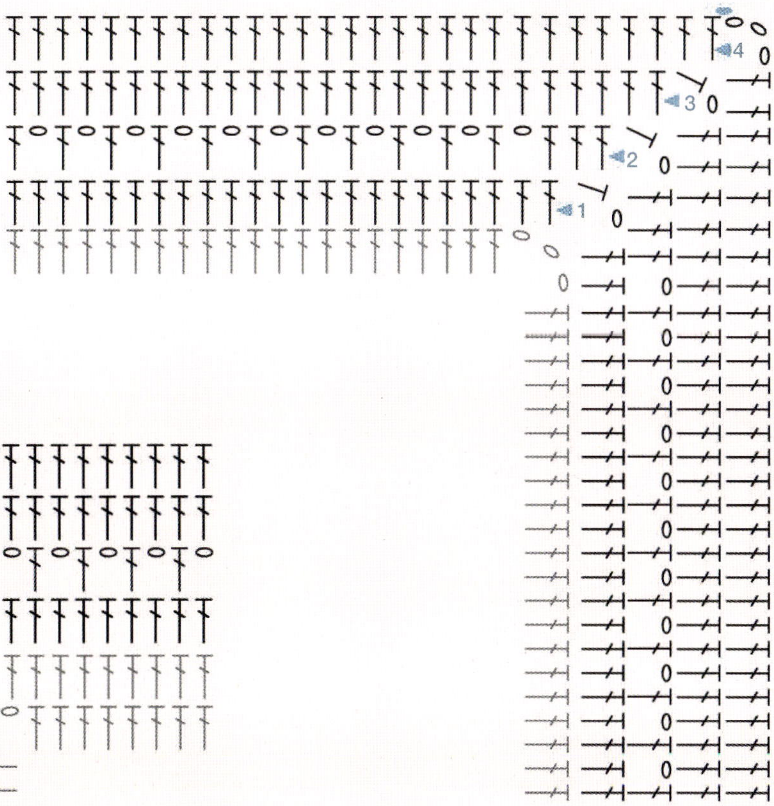

Joining Chart

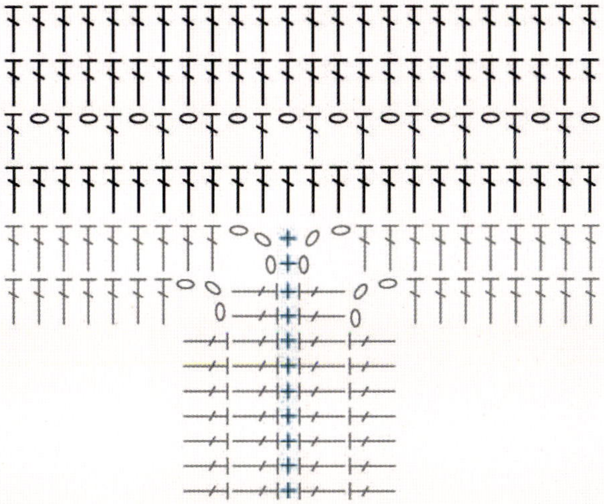

Acknowledgements

Thank you to our husbands and children, for your patience and for listening to all our ideas, sharing your thoughts on colours and patterns, and coming up with the names for our designs.

Thank you, G. Brouwer & Zn, for sponsoring the yarn.

Thank you to the testers Ilona, Denise, Heleen, Saskia, Marly, Martal and Elly, for carefully crocheting, reading and reviewing all the patterns and charts.

Thank you, Kosmos, for helping to make our dream come true and for the faith you have in us!

Thank you to Marissa van Roon for the wonderful photos and the fun we had shooting them.

Thank you, Johanna, for letting us use your beautiful farmhouse in Zoutelande. Facebook huisjeindepolder.

And last but not least, thank you to Bram. You are a fantastic 'office dog', giving us breaks from work and making us laugh at your antics. We needed that sometimes so that we could return later to our drawings and patterns with fresh eyes.

Take a look at our website at:

www.haakplein.com

for more inspiration. There are still so many wonderful things to discover!